THE ILLUSTRATED HISTORY OF THE HAMBURGER

Hamburger Heaven

JEFFREY TENNYSON

HYPERION • NEW YORK

D E D I C A T E D

to my loving and supportive family, Betty, Don, Lisa, and Rob Tennyson,
and to a great friend and inspiration Jay Brown.

Library of Congress Cataloging-in-Publication Data

Tennyson, Jeffrey.
Hamburger Heaven / Jeffrey Tennyson.—1st ed.
p.   cm.
ISBN 0-7868-8080-5
1. Hamburgers (Sandwiches)—History.
2. Hamburgers (Sandwiches)—Collectables.
3. Fast food restaurants—United States—
History.   I. Title.
GT2868.5.T46   1993 338.4'76479573—dc20
93-11054
CIP

First Paperback Edition
10 9 8 7 6 5 4 3 2 1

Book Design: Jeffrey Tennyson
Cover Illustration: David Willardson

CONTENTS

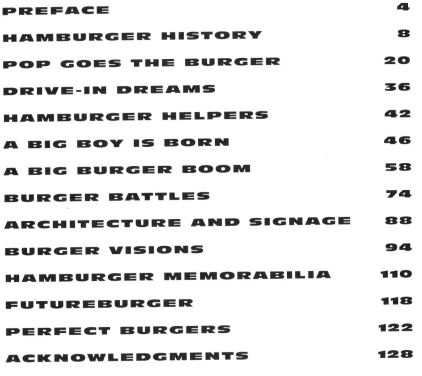

PREFACE

WHITE MANNA, HACKENSACK, NEW JERSEY, AS PAINTED BY JOHN BAEDER, 1974.

Lauded for its convenience and versatility as either snack or entrée, and labeled as both a cultural icon and a cliché, the hamburger—this omnipresent beef-between-bun creation—is a meaty, multifaceted phenomenon. And if a society is what it eats, then a thoughtful, entertaining look at the hamburger is an illumination of an important sociocultural institution.

Never mind apple pie. (When did you crave it last?) Forget about hot dogs. (Burgers surpassed franks in popularity back in the Forties.) The hamburger is hands-down our all-time favorite food. The average American consumes nearly thirty pounds of hamburger a year—three burgers per person, per week,

"HAMBURGER HEAVEN" BY JEFFREY TENNYSON. ACRYLIC ON CANVAS.

totaling 38 billion burgers annually, which when placed end to end would form a heavenly chain of hamburgers 1.8 million miles long. A celestial vision to be sure!

While hamburgers today are considered just another necessity of life, many of us recall fondly our adolescent introduction to the joys of hamburger cuisine. Burgers were the reason to cook-out, eat-out, or drive-in. Not only was the mid-twentieth century the golden age of television (we loved Lucy), it was also the postwar culture in full bloom, and a glorious time for hamburgers.

The first burger I ever tasted was at Thomas's Drive-In in Niles, Michigan. Thomas's was a haven for hamburger lovers, and it was there that our family sought comfort food on Mom's weekly respite from the kitchen. When we all piled into Dad's big shiny Buick and headed for Thomas's, it was a major event. On any given evening it seemed as though at least half of the local population had been thinking along the same lines. At Thomas's the customers had the option of remaining in their cars, where a perky young carhop would tend to their every need, or sitting inside at a glitter-flecked vinyl booth equipped with a table-top jukebox. Dion and the Belmonts and Sam

SPEEDY, MCDONALD'S ORIGINAL MASCOT, STILL LIGHTS UP THE NIGHT IN DOWNEY, CALIFORNIA.

Cooke would provide the dinner music. Girls with ponytails were everywhere.

Although there certainly were other items on the menu, everyone seemed to order the same thing: hamburgers! Near delirium at the thought of chowing down on this strange and exotic cuisine (it was so much better than meatloaf!), my brother and I could hardly sit still in anticipation. Soon our waitress would deliver bountiful burger baskets brimming with hot, juicy cheeseburgers (deluxe in every way), crispy, fresh-cut fries, and big, drippy chocolate malts (too much for the glass to hold, so the extra was reserved on the side in its steel mixing flask). All were strategically placed in front of us on the boomerang-patterned Formica—just inches from our widened eyes and lips. I can't recall a home-cooked meal ever achieving quite the same effect.

This entire hamburger-related ritual—"dinner at the drive-in"—had a magical aura about it, and to many who experienced it, the glow (like the taste of a good burger) still lingers.

By the time Thomas's succumbed to fire in the late Sixties, its magic had already begun to fade, as Niles, like the rest of the nation, entered the era of the self-service restaurant. These would be dark days for drive-ins, but a heady time for hamburgers. A revolution in 15-cent hamburgers begun by two brothers from California by the name of McDonald would sweep across the country and capture the fancy of a nation in a big hurry. To a population seeking faster food and speedy service, handy hamburgers would always be the perfect match.

This is the panoramic story of that match made in heaven. It's an enlightening trip from drive-ins to drive-thrus, from White Castles to Golden Arches. It's a dazzling vision of Burger Americana that will leave you exhilarated, and probably a little hungry.

BURGER-A-GO-GO BY PAUL ROGERS (FACING PAGE).

HAMBURGER HISTORY

In the beginning . . . there were no burgers. History tells us that man evolved from an ape-like tree-dweller who came down from his lofty habitat thirty-five million years ago in search of additional foodstuffs. Either he was losing interest in the tree cuisine that had sustained him for several thousand years, or, as some theorize, a shortage of this food brought on by a drying out of the Pliocene forests forced his descent to the grasslands to forage. Either way, he could hardly have been disappointed by the bounty that awaited him on the lower level. On the ground, his diet was expanded to include a variety of tasty new items including lizards, porcupines, moles, insects, and grubs.

This creature, the *Australopithicus afarensis,* was not highly evolved; in fact, it would take several million years for him to learn to stand up straight. Living in the grassland, he became a meat-eater and a family man.

While on the ground, an upright posture and bipedal (two-legged) stance was eventually adopted, the result of which was to free his hands for the creation and utilization of tools of stone. With these hands he fashioned the

WISHFUL THINKING. OUR ANCIENT ANCESTOR, *AUSTRALO-PITHICUS,* LIVED A BURGERLESS LIFE, BUT MAY HAVE BEEN THE WORLD'S FIRST BEEFEATER.

PALEOLITHIC CAVE PAINTINGS DISCOVERED IN LASCAUX, FRANCE, REVEAL EARLY MAN'S PREDILECTION FOR THE BOVINE SPECIES.

most important implement in his tool kit: the stone "chopping tool."

The existence of these stone choppers and mashers, and the wooden spears found among them, clearly illustrates the importance of meat in the diet of these prehistoric men. They still didn't have burgers, but they'd come a long way.

Before long, rock-smashing, tool-forming activities would accidentally send a spark into a bed of dried grasses, igniting a fire and searing the fresh ration of meat, which had been stored fortuitously close by. What must have

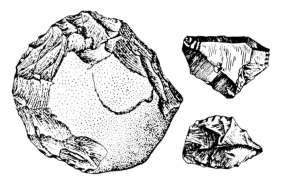

BEFORE THE MODERN MEAT GRINDER, PRIMITIVE STONE TOOLS SUCH AS THESE WERE USED TO CHOP THE STEAK.

HOMO ERECTUS WAS A SKILLFUL HUNTER AND MASTER OF THE OUTDOOR BARBECUE.

BEEF BONES WERE AMONG THE RELICS EXCAVATED FROM AN EGYPTIAN TOMB DATED IN THE THIRD MILLENNIUM B.C. COULD BURGERS HAVE BEEN FAR BEHIND?

appeared initially as a disaster was, as we now know, a major gastronomic breakthrough. This chance discovery of fire would lead our ancestor, in short order, to the special joys of the outdoor barbecue. Man was now capable of capturing, chopping, and cooking his food.

Our apeman, *Homo habilis,* evolved into *Homo erectus,* a five-foot cave dweller. We can discern by examining the bones that littered his caves that as small as he was in stature, he was a skillful hunter and a heavy meat-eater with an affinity for venison, antelope, and bison—the bovine predecessor and

CONTRARY TO THE ARTIST'S (MIS)CONCEPTION ABOVE, RUSSIAN BURGER-EATERS OF THE MIDDLE AGES HAD YET TO DISCOVER THE GLORY OF GARNISH. THEIR ALL-BEEF BURGERS WERE JUST THAT.

distant relative of today's beef cattle.

By 75,000 B.C., an even larger-brained successor to *Homo erectus* appeared on the scene. This race of *Homo sapiens,* the Neanderthal, has been unjustly stereotyped as simple-minded and brutish. Although clumsy in appearance, he was actually an advanced breed of human. Findings indicate that the Neanderthals occupying the Zagros Mountains of Iran between thirty and fifty thousand years ago experienced consistently good hunting, and favored a particular breed of wild cattle which was a hearty cousin of our mod-

ern day burger-bearing species.

Recorded "Burger History" began in the thirteenth century when wild, nomadic horsemen overran much of Asia and Eastern Europe and simultaneously laid the groundwork for the hamburger.

The various tribes of Tartary were predominantly of Mongolian and Turkish descent, and inhabited a large expanse of territory stretching from the Dnieper River in European Russia to the Chinese coast on the Sea of Japan. These notoriously rowdy riders were also hearty meat-eaters who loved their steaks

raw. Known for their fierce territorial conquests and raiding missions, legend has it that as they pushed their way across Russia and Eastern Europe, it was their custom to cut a fillet from a conquered cow, place it under their ''saddle'' for safekeeping, and ride off into the horizon in search of ever more exciting macho maraudings. By the time the dinner hour rolled around, the steak had been conveniently tenderized beneath the pounding saddle, and was ready to be served—minced and uncooked.

Whether or not this ''Tribal Tartar Saddle Scenario'' is the historically correct origin of the chopped raw beef dish now known as Steak Tartare, we do know that this traditional dish, later prepared by shredding the raw steaks with a dull knife, was favored by the nomads as much for its quickness in preparation as for its fresh and tasty tenderness.

As the territorial influence of the Tartars grew, the inhabitants of the Baltic provinces of Finland, Estonia, and Latvia were introduced to this dish, and they developed a fondness for it seasoned with salt, pepper, and onion juice. Indeed, it was considered a great delicacy. Today's hamburger is a direct de-

scendant of Steak Tartare.

By the eighteenth century, Hamburg was the largest seaport in Europe. It enjoyed special status and trading privileges with several Russian ports. Over time, German merchant sailors crossing the Baltic Sea sampled the local fare in these Russian cities and developed a taste for the popular raw steak they encountered ashore.

When the men returned home to Hamburg, they brought with them a ravenous appetite for their favorite new food. Resourceful German chefs experimented with variations, sometimes adding a raw egg to enrich the patties. Finally, in a magic moment of gargantuan gastronomic import, the meat was cooked lightly with chopped onions and the flavor was enhanced significantly.

In the early nineteenth century, Hamburg was the major point of departure for German immigrants bound for the United States. In addition to their worldly possessions, they brought with them their native dishes, including the popular broiled chopped steak. This variation of the original raw recipe would soon become known in the New World as Hamburg Style Steak, and was first popularized by

IN 1907 "HAMBURGER GENE" MCINTURFF BEGAN SELLING HAMBURGERS FOR A NICKEL APIECE (TWENTY-FIVE FOR A DOLLAR) FROM A SMALL WAGON AT THE CORNER OF FIRST AND MAIN STREETS IN HUTCHINSON, KANSAS, AND CONTINUED TO DO SO FOR TWENTY-FOUR YEARS. HIS HAMBURGERS—SERVED WITH PICKLE AND ONION—WERE LEGENDARY.

immigrants settling in the Ohio River Valley.

Meanwhile, on America's eastern seaboard, "steak cooked in the Hamburg style" made its New York City debut when German sailors who patronized eating stands along the piers in New York Harbor made their special requests to the dockside short-order cooks. From these modest beginnings, Hamburg Steak gradually made its way onto the menus of American restaurants, and by 1896 made its first cookbook appearance in Fannie Farmer's *Boston Cooking-School Cookbook*.

In what has frequently been mistaken for

<DELMONICO'S>
RESTAURANT.
494·PEARL·STREET.

BILL OF FARE.

Cup Tea or Coffee,	1	Pork Chops,		4
Bowl " "	2	Pork and Beans,		4
Crullers,	1	Sausages,		4
Soup,	2	Puddings,		4
Fried or Stewed Liver,	3	Liver and Bacon,		5
" " Heart,	3	Roast Beef or Veal,		5
Hash,	3	Roast Mutton,		5
Pies,	4	Veal Cutlet,		5
Half Pie,	2	Chicken Stew,		5
Beef or Mutton Stew,	4	Fried Eggs,		5
Corn Beef and Cabbage,	4	Ham and Eggs,		10
Pigs Head " "	4	Hamburger Steak,		10
Fried Fish,	4	Roast Chicken,		10
Beef Steak,	4			

Regular Dinner 12 Cents.

"HAMBURGER STEAKS" ARE FEATURED ON THIS 1834 MENU FROM NEW YORK'S FABLED DELMONICO'S, THEIR EARLIEST DOCUMENTED AMERICAN APPEARANCE.

DINERS, AND THEIR SMALLER COUNTERPARTS "DINETTES," SPECIALIZED IN THE SHORT-ORDER MEAL. THE WHITE STAR WAS MANUFACTURED BY THE KULLMAN COMPANY IN THE LATE 1940S.

AT THE TURN OF THE CENTURY, VENDORS WITH LUNCH CARTS LIKE THIS ONE NEAR BELLEVUE, WASHINGTON, HELPED POPULARIZE THE STILL UNFAMILIAR HAMBURGER SANDWICH.

the birthday of the burger, the Walla Walla (Washington) *Union* included one of the first known references to Hamburg Steak in its January 5, 1889, edition when an amused reporter related how the patrons dining at a local restaurant were asked to make their dinner selection from one of the following: "porkchopbeefsteakhamandeggshamburgsteakorliver." Even if this *had* been the first documented appearance of Hamburg Steak (which it wasn't), it certainly didn't refer to its illustrious hand-held descendant, which had yet to be devised.

In 1884, five years prior to the Walla Walla affair, the Boston *Journal* quoted a restaurant cook's unique approach to chicken preparation: "We take a chicken and boil it. And when

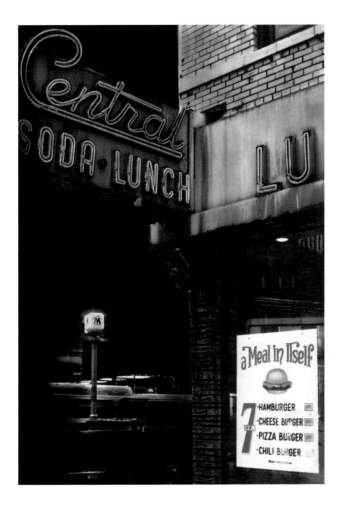

KEN LASSEN STILL SERVES BURGERS AT LOUIS' LUNCH IN NEW HAVEN, CONNECTICUT, WHERE, HE CLAIMS, HIS GRANDFATHER LOUIS (PICTURED) DEVISED AMERICA'S FIRST HAMBURGER SANDWICH.

THE CORNER SODA FOUNTAIN WAS AN EARLY SOURCE OF A QUICK LUNCH AND A RELIABLE BURGER.

it's cold we cut it up as they do to make Hamburg Steak.'' But both of these citings take place nearly fifty years after the first appearance of the dish. Its debut was traced to the 1834 menu of New York's fabled Delmonico's steak house.

But a Hamburg Steak is not a hamburger. The great experiment that began several centuries earlier with the culinary quirks of the Tartars would continue its evolution toward absolute perfection.

We know that at some historic moment the Hamburg Steak patty acquired its top and bottom layers, and sprung forth as a hand-held hamburger sandwich, thus closing the door at last on the era of the bunless burger.

In the late 1800s, American cities in the East and Midwest experienced a phenomenal growth fueled by rapid industrial expansion, and a swelling immigrant labor force. This new breed of working-class laborer, short on time and on a strict budget, found it more convenient and economical to grab a quick bite in ''short order'' from lunchrooms and street vendors rather than travel home for a noontime meal. In 1856, *Harper's Weekly* observed: ''They swallow, but they don't eat; and like a boa constrictor, they bolt everything.''

One of the earliest caterers to the eat-and-run crowd, and a forerunner of today's fast-food dispensaries, was the lunch cart or lunch wagon. An 1872 horse-drawn innovation that roamed the city streets offering a variety of bargain-priced victuals, these urban chuck wagons often lingered near factories where the hungry masses were in no short supply. Hamburgers were often sold two for a nickel.

Eventually these carts evolved into grand and gleaming dining cars, or "diners." Reminiscent of railroad dining cars and still popular today, many diners continue to fry up magnificently messy hamburgers.

The popularity of these factory diners surged at the turn of the century, and so did

CHARLIE NAGREEN'S SUPPORTERS IN SEYMOUR, WISCONSIN, MAINTAIN THAT HE INVENTED THE HAMBURGER IN 1885 AT THE AGE OF FIFTEEN, SERVING THEM AT THE COUNTY FAIRGROUNDS. HE'S SEEN HERE STILL DISHING THEM OUT IN 1950.

another American eating institution: the soda fountain. An innovation of the Civil War years, when drugstore counters began serving mixtures of soda water and sweet syrup, stopping at the soda fountain had become a favorite pastime by 1900. In 1874 a fountain operator in Philadelphia ran out of syrup and substituted ice cream, thereby creating the world's first ice cream soda. Americans were crazy for this concoction, and by 1908 there were nearly seventy-five thousand fountains in operation. Recognizing a need for fast fare and refreshment, many fountain operators began to serve light meals along with sundaes and sodas. Menus typically included soup, sandwiches, and hamburgers.

As burger purveyors, these soda fountains evolved into another familiar quick-dining establishment: the luncheonette. Local retailers and five-and-dime variety stores such as Woolworth's added luncheonettes with counters and stools, to the satisfaction of those in search of the hasty and the tasty.

Perhaps one of the most enduring of all eating establishments born in the late 1800s is the down home, hole-in-the-wall, "greasy spoon." These tiny unpretentious "stool lunch" eateries proliferated. Often they remained open throughout the night, offering an oasis of refuge to those who congregated counterside for a cup of fresh-ground coffee, some friendly conversation, and a fabulous hamburger sandwich or two (also freshly ground).

In these plain and simple six-stool luncheonettes, the hamburger was destined to come into its own. Louis' Lunch is one such example that survives today in New Haven, Connecticut. It claims to be the birthplace of the hamburger. Owner Ken Lassen—grandson of the original owner, Louis—boasts that in 1900 his grandfather invented the burger when, on a moment's notice, he filled the request for a quick sandwich by hastily forming a patty of thinly sliced steak trimmings, which he served between two slices of bread. This hamburger (America's first?) is still served at Louis' Lunch today, and is prepared on the original "vertical broiler," which Louis invented.

Another important outlet for early burgers was the amusement park and county fair concession stand.

Seymour, Wisconsin, alleges that one of its home boys, Charlie Nagreen, gave birth to the hamburger in 1885 (at the age of fifteen!), when he delivered the world's first from behind his ox-drawn concession stand at the Outgamie County Fair. As they tell it, Charlie was selling ground beef to hungry fairgoers, but he had a problem. His customers wanted to stroll about the fairgrounds as they ate and they needed a convenient way to carry their lunch with them. Charlie solved the problem by placing the beef between bread slices, "and calling it a hamburger." A fairground fixture for sixty-five years, "hamburger Charlie" fried his burgers in butter, serving them up to the folks who sought him out not only to eat his famous creation, but also to get a close look at the legend himself.

None of this sits too well with the Menches family of Akron, Ohio, the direct descendants of Frank Menches who, according to an obituary in the October 5, 1951, edition of the Los Angeles *Daily News*, was "widely credited with inventing the hamburger" while a concessionaire at the Akron County Fair in 1892. "When he nearly ran out of sausage, in an effort to please his customers, he ground it up and sold it as a cooked meat patty." Judy Kismits, the great-granddaughter of Frank Menches, corrects the obituary: "Actually, Frank and his brother Charles were well

DESCENDANTS OF CONCESSIONAIRE FRANK MENCHES ARE CONVINCED THAT HE ACCIDENTALLY INVENTED THE HAMBURGER WHEN HE RAN OUT OF SAUSAGE.

DAILY NEWS, Los Angeles
FRIDAY, OCT. 5, 1951   11

Hamburger inventor dies

AKRON, O., Oct. 5.- (UP) - Concessionaire Frank Menches, who is credited with "inventing" the hamburger, died here today at the age of 86.

Menches ended his active life as concessionaire for county fairs here in 1938, but not until after he had left his mark on the gastronomic habits of the nation.

Before the turn of the century, Menches entered the concession business. At the Summit County (Akron) fair in 1892, Menches nearly ran out of sausage. In an effort to please his customers, he ground up a sausage and sold it as a cooked meat patty.

It was unexplainably named "hamburger" about two years later.

That concoction, plus his introduction and manufacture of ice cream cones here from the world's fair of 1903, brought Menches a small fortune.

INTERSTATE FAIR
York, Pa

Hamburg Used From
JOE BURY'S STAND
5 Days Fair

1936 ....1,285 lbs.
1937 ....3,350 lbs.
1938 ....5,473 lbs.
1939 ....8,950 lbs.
1940 ....12,200 lbs.

JOE BURY'S *Famous* HAMBURGERS

WE SERVE *Ahrens Quality* MEATS

WE SERVE *Ahrens Quality* MEATS

61,000 HAMBURGERS—24 HEAD CATTLE BUTCHERED, GROUND UP, PADDED AND GRILLED AND SLAPPED BETWEEN 5,000 DOZ. ROLLS. THE ONIONS AND KETCHUP USED WOULD LAST AN ORDINARY FAMILY A LIFETIME. THERE WERE 12,200 LBS. OF BEEF USED, 3,250 LBS. MORE THAN 1939.

IN A REMARKABLE FEAT, CONCESSIONAIRE EXTRAORDINAIRE JOE BURY SERVED 61,000 OF HIS FAMOUS HAMBURGERS DURING HIS FIVE-DAY STINT AT THE 1940 STATE FAIR IN YORK, PENNSYLVANIA.

known for their popular pork sausage sandwiches, but the butcher had been unable to provide them with sausage that day (a heat wave and high humidity had precluded the slaughter), so they substituted ground beef as a last resort." The brothers agreed that the ground beef lacked the zest of their sausage sandwiches and needed help . . . in a hurry. They did a bit of experimenting and eventually settled on a mixture of seasonings that "remains a well-guarded family secret to this day." An account of these events published in 1970, in the book *Tanbark and Tinsel* by John C. Kudson, was drawn from interviews with the elder Frank Menches. He also invented the ice cream cone, but that's another story. . . .

Further fueling the fiery father-of-the-burger debate is the oft-noted appearance of the hamburger at the 1904 World's Fair in St. Louis, where a reporter for the New York *Tribune* reported it to be "the innovation of a food vendor on the pike (midway)." Most gastro-

nomic volumes cite this event as the first documented burger debut. Coincidentally, Frank Menches was in attendance at the fair. Judy says that it's quite possible that he was the busy vendor hawking hamburgers.

Tell that to the Texas offspring of Fletcher Davis who argue rather convincingly that their Great-grampa Fletcher "Old Dave" Davis was the nameless burger concessionaire referred to in the New York *Tribune* article. Old Dave, they say, invented the hamburger in his modest Athens, Texas, lunch counter where he developed quite a reputation for his fried ground-beef patties slathered with hot mustard, topped with a slice of Bermuda onion, and tucked between his homemade bread.

Davis attended the World's Fair in St. Louis, with wife Ciddy, and operated a sandwich concession—selling burgers—on the midway. Based on information provided by Fletcher's relatives, both *Restaurants and Institutions* magazine and *USA Today* assert that Old Dave

LUNCH-COUNTERS WITH STOOLS PROVIDED A DECENT MEAL ON A WORKINGMAN'S BUDGET. IN 1932 THIS GREASY SPOON'S MENU INCLUDED 10-CENT "HAMBURGS."

was indeed the man in question. Another account describes his burgers as having "caused a sensation at the 1904 fair." So maybe Old Dave wasn't the first (Frank and Charlie were dishing them up in the 1800s), but he certainly deserves a bit of credit for getting great press, and sharing so much with so many.

The burger daddy dispute rages on to this day, and will never be resolved to everyone's complete satisfaction. Perhaps we should applaud all participants, and acknowledge our eternal indebtedness to their combined efforts. We will never be able to establish with absolute certainty which of these visionaries was the first to envision the Hamburg Steak as a succulent sandwich. The fact is, the birth of the burger was a process of natural perfection—evolving gloriously and spontaneously—it appears to have sizzled to life in a number of historic locations at approximately the same time. A brilliant idea whose time had *finally* come.

IT WAS WIDELY REPORTED THAT FLETCHER DAVIS'S BURGERS CAUSED QUITE A SENSATION WHEN THEY WERE SERVED AT THE 1904 WORLD'S FAIR IN ST. LOUIS.

POP GOES THE BURGER
CASTLES COVER THE LAND

In 1916 in Wichita, Kansas, J. Walter Anderson set out to perfect a moister, more flavorful hamburger. His idea—to flatten the unwieldy mound of meat into small patties, mash in shredded onions, then sear them quickly at high temperature on both sides—enhanced the flavor significantly by sealing in the succulent juices.

Prior to Anderson's efforts in the name of burger perfection, hamburgers, like most sandwiches, were generally served between two slices of bread. Walter's unique approach, however, called for placing freshly baked *buns* on top of the steaming patties to absorb the flavor of the beef and onions. Reporting in a 1973 edition of the Wichita *Eagle,* writer Don Granger asserts that "it is very likely that Walter Anderson invented the hamburger bun."

Anderson's new "flattened" burger variation drew raves when he tested it out on the patrons of the restaurant where he was employed as a short-order cook. Not long after,

HAMBURGER PIONEERS WALT ANDERSON AND BILLY INGRAM, FOUNDERS OF AMERICA'S FIRST HAMBURGER CHAIN, IN FRONT OF THEIR TENTH "CASTLE." C. 1927

THE FIRST WHITE CASTLE OPENED IN WICHITA IN 1921.

20

AN ELEGANT IMAGE FROM THE FORTIES OFFERS SOUND ADVICE.

LET US DO YOU A FLAVOR
TRY OUR CHEESEBURGER

"Put them in cartons and a bag --- We're having Hamburgers for dinner tonight"

White Castle
HAMBURGERS
Buy 'em by the "Sack"

from an Idea to A NATIONAL INSTITUTION -through constant striving to improve

White Castle HAMBURGERS
BUY 'EM BY THE "SACK"

You Can Eat With Confidence If It's a

White Castle HAMBURGER
Buy 'em by the "Sack"

An Ideal 25¢ — SUPPER — 25¢
Before or After the Show

White Castle
A NATIONAL INSTITUTION

he converted a trolley car to his own five-stool lunch counter, and devised a special grill (the forerunner of today's flat institutional griddle) large enough to accommodate an anticipated booming burger business.

Anderson recognized that many people were apprehensive when it came to eating out, with legitimate concerns in regard to food quality and cleanliness. Greasy spoons were, after all, *greasy*, and at that time, there were no strict regulations monitoring the quality of hamburger meat. To put his customers' fears to rest he installed the grill behind the counter, where his burgers were freshly ground and prepared to order in full view of his curious clientele.

An article in a local newspaper quoted Walter's wife Martha on his first day of operation: "He stood on the sidewalk in front of his diner, and yelled, 'Hamburgers—a nickel apiece.' By three o'clock he'd sold all his hamburgers, and went back to Dye's for more meat."

The quality of this refined breed of burger was virtually assured by its creator's insistence that the fresh meat and buns be delivered twice daily. The public deemed his flavorful onion-steamed creation irresistible. When Walt used the slogan "Buy 'em by the sack," his customers gobbled them with gusto.

WHITE CASTLE MASTERFULLY PROMOTED THE BENEFITS OF BURGERS IN COLORFUL POSTERS AND ON ADJUSTABLE PAPER CAPS (TOP), WHICH THEY INVENTED IN THE 1920S.

BEFORE WORLD WAR II, WHITE CASTLE EMPLOYED MALE PERSONNEL EXCLUSIVELY.

In 1920, Anderson opened two additional hamburger outlets, and in 1921, teaming his resources with a local real estate investor by the name of Edgar Waldo "Billy" Ingram, he opened a fourth. This newest location was constructed of cement blocks ruggedly cast to resemble rocks, and sported a castle motif complete with rooftop battlements and a turret. The structure was then painted white, and, at the suggestion of Ingram, the words "White Castle Hamburgers 5 cents" were added to the exterior. The name White Castle was chosen to signify purity and cleanliness. The castle motif, inspired by the famous Chicago Water Tower, was meant to evoke the image of strength, stability, and permanence. The concept worked.

Later that year, four more White Castles opened

CHICAGO'S WATER TOWER INSPIRED WHITE CASTLE'S MEDIEVAL ARCHITECTURAL MOTIF.

their doors in Wichita. By standardizing a formula and implementing it with steadfast consistency, this winning combination of distinctive architecture, and spotless interiors, all built to serve an enigmatic little nickel hamburger with seemingly unlimited appeal, proved to be astoundingly popular. By 1930 the "White Castle System" had grown to over one hundred units in ten states.

In 1930, in an effort to promote the nutritional benefits of habitual hamburger consumption (some mothers still hadn't been won over), White Castle implemented a scientific study, in which (in the words of the co-founder, Ingram): "We arranged for a medical student to live for 13 weeks on nothing but White Castle Hamburgers and water. The student maintained good health throughout the three-month period, and was eating twenty to twenty-four hamburgers a day during the last few weeks. A food scientist signed a report that a normal, healthy child could eat nothing

but our hamburgers and water, and fully develop all its physical and mental faculties if we were to do two things: increase the percentage of calcium in the buns to aid in the development of bone structure, and maintain a specific proportion of bun and patty to provide the correct balance of proteins, carbohydrates, and fat." Needless to say, they gladly complied with the recommendations.

White Castle successfully promoted its product by constantly upgrading the image of the hamburger. It was also the first establishment to hawk hamburgers via well-conceived newspaper advertising campaigns urging consumers to "buy 'em by the sack." This promotional blitz proved so effective that it necessitated the development of a special cardboard carton for each burger to eliminate smashed burgers at the bottom of the bag.

Due in large part to the success of its widespread hamburger promotion, White Castle is credited with inventing and popularizing the "fast food" hamburger. It became the nation's first hamburger chain, and pioneered the concept of standardized image, menu, and service, and was the prototype for all of today's modern fast-food restaurants.

The folks at White Castle are also responsible for the invention of those adjustable

WHITE CASTLE'S TREND-SETTING BABY BURGERS. A SACK OF TWENTY PACKED IN SPECIAL CRUSH-PROOF CARTONS COULD BE HAD FOR A DOLLAR.

(OPPOSITE PAGE) WHITE CASTLE WENT TO GREAT LENGTHS TO WIN OVER WARY MOTHERS WHO, IN THE EARLY DAYS OF THE HAMBURGER, EXPRESSED CONCERN OVER MEAT QUALITY.

DOES SHE LIKE IT?

You answer that one

paper hats that became an integral part of the image and uniform of many a sandwich server. Originally conceived as both "a sanitary measure and to improve appearance" they were devised after much experimentation with the folding of paper napkins.

In 1933 Mr. Anderson retired as president of White Castle and Billy Ingram continued to oversee the thriving operation of the family-owned organization. In the early Thirties, with yet another trailblazing innovation, the chain replaced the fresh ground beef with "modern" prefrozen patties. A dubious development to be sure, but one that—in the words of Ingram—had certain obvious advantages: "The hamburger could be placed on the griddle while still frozen and thus give our customers the added assurance of quality."

By 1956 the growing White Castle system announced that it had served 91,566,342 hamburgers in that year alone—more than any other organization of restaurants in the United States—and they were hoping to break the one hundred million mark in 1957. A typical modern White Castle restaurant was capable of producing three thousand hamburgers per hour, and many customers were reportedly "eating a dozen in one sitting."

About this time they altered their time-honored recipe ever so slightly by patenting a process that added five equally spaced holes to the patties, an "improvement" that was found to "cook the patty faster, and allow for better steaming of the bun." This hole-y hamburger patty is in use to this day.

White Castles are still plentiful and popular, with over two hundred fifty restaurants located primarily in the Midwest and Southeast.

TODAY, DEVOTEES OF WHITE CASTLE HAMBURGERS
FONDLY REFER TO THEM AS SLIDERS AND BELLY BOMBERS.

You can be sure if it's fresh frozen…

— and White Castle all-Beef Hamburgers are.

—sure that White Castle's 100% beef patties are kept at the peak of their perfection by flash freezing

—sure that the good beef flavor has been kept for you.

SLIGHTLY AHEAD OF ITS TIME, WHITE CASTLE SWITCHED TO "MODERN" FROZEN PATTIES IN THE 1930S.

Devotees of the 2 ounce, 2½ inch square, onion-soaked, hole-poked burgers are notoriously obsessed with the sandwiches, which they often lovingly refer to as "sliders" or "belly bombers." Syndicated columnist Bob Greene maintains, "If you grew up on White Castle hamburgers, no other fast-food burger will do." Apparently there are millions who share his viewpoint. Amazing true tales of White Castle addiction are in no short supply:

A pregnant Las Vegas woman who developed an intense craving for sliders, but could find no local supplier, was greatly relieved when her father-in-law shipped her one hundred frozen "castles," which she was able to heat and eat at home. "They were gone well within a week and a half," she recalled later.

By 1982, White Castle was shipping an average of ten thousand hamburgers per week to feed the needs of those no longer residing on its home turf. The same year, it implemented a toll-free phone number for ordering the frozen, precooked hamburgers, packed in dry ice, and delivered anywhere within the continental United States within forty-eight hours. For many it was a dream come true. Imagine! Belly bombers—just a phone call away. What will those innovators think of next? Would you believe . . . frozen White Castles in your friendly grocer's freezer? In 1987, White Castle became the first burger chain to market its hamburgers in the supermarket.

Not everyone craves the taste of the slider. Even hard-core addicts often describe it as an acquired taste. And there are some, admittedly, who never get beyond the first bite. The White Castle hamburger exists as a modern-day reminder of what hamburgers were in their infancy. Simple and basic, with the emphasis on the beef. Burgers weren't born with lettuce and tomato.

From its inception in the early Twenties, the extraordinary success of White Castle instantly begat a host of imitators who bor-

rowed more than just their proven formula of standardization. The influence of White Castle became immediately and profoundly apparent, as the number of copycat competitors proliferated throughout the Thirties, Forties, and Fifties. Attempting to duplicate White Castle's success, many restaurateurs arrived at glaringly similar names and architectural motifs for their eateries. Frequently the word

"white" was incorporated into the name of the establishment, and towers and castle motifs became quite common. White—which had originally been chosen by the White Castle founder because of its clean, pure connotations—was evolving into a bit of a phenomenon in itself, as it continued to be associated with the quick-service hamburger "systems."

There were White Towers, White Huts, White

In 1937, this gleaming Philadelphia White Tower interior was obviously a wonderful setting for "the best meal of the year."

The first White Tower buildings duplicated White Castle's medieval motifs, but in the Thirties they embraced art deco and streamlined modernism. This 1938 jewel was on Tremont Street in Boston.

Mannas, White Clocks, White Domes, White Diamonds, White Crests, White Cups, White Palaces, White Taverns, White Midgets, and White Spots. There were also Royal Castles, Kings Castles, Blue Castles, Silver Castles, Blue Towers, and Red Beacons.

The most obvious and successful of the White Castle imitators, the White Tower restaurant chain, was founded in Milwaukee, Wisconsin, in 1926. Like White Castles, White

Towers were often strategically situated on busy street corners in cities, usually within walking distance of subways, buses, and trolley lines.

Borrowing the medieval motif, the compulsion for pristine cleanliness, and just about everything else, White Tower also grew to become one of the largest restaurant chains of the 1930s with their enormously popular nickel hamburgers and famous cup of java. Like White Castle, White Tower developed a brisk take-out business for their menu mainstay with their mottoes: "Buy a bagful," and "A lunch in a bag in a jiffy."

White Tower would eventually move away from the Medieval exteriors, adopting a slick, streamlined, modernistic style designed by architect Charles Johnson. In contrast to White Castle's policy of promoting their burgers through advertising, White Tower believed that the impression made by their glistening enamel building facades—spectacularly illuminated in the nighttime sky, along with the irresistible fragrance of burgers sizzling on the grill, was all the enticement anyone required. This was indeed the case until well into the 1960s, when the lack of competitive advertising, and the steadfast decay of the neighborhoods where they were located, undoubtedly led to White Tower's decline.

Several other early hamburger chains achieved some measure of their success by duplicating White Castle's methods in whole

A REGIONAL FAVORITE TO THIS DAY, THE LITTLE TAVERN CHAIN BEGAN SERVING THEIR 5-CENT ONION-SPICED BURGERS IN LOUISVILLE IN 1927.

DETAILS FROM RESTAURANT CHINA (CIRCA 1930) ILLUSTRATE A FEW OF THE INNUMERABLE NICKEL HAMBURGER "SYSTEMS" INSPIRED BY THE GREAT WHITE CASTLES.

ROYAL CASTLE AND KRYSTAL WERE BOTH FOUNDED ON THE PERVASIVE "BUY-A-BAG-OF-BURGERS" PHILOSOPHY OF THE 1930S.

or in part. These Castle copycats include The Royal Castle chain which was founded in Miami in 1938, and peaked in 1970 with fifty hamburger outlets. Maid-Rite Hamburgs began in 1926 as a humble walk-up burger stand in Muscatine, Iowa, with a dirt floor and no running water. According to owner Clayton Blue, "The name 'Maid-Rite' was chosen to imply wholesomeness and pureness." Still doing business in twelve states today, their specialty—a double-ground-loose-meat sandwich—is steamed in secret seasonings, and is so tender and delicate a creation that "it must be served with a spoon to pick up the (meat) spillover." A popular western chain called Rockybuilt was born in Denver in 1936, and The Krystal Shop hamburger stands opened their doors in Chattanooga in 1932.

Like a number of their predecessors in the field, Krystal Shops were prefabricated, movable units of white porcelain. In a departure from historical associations with castles,

AS ALL TRUE BURGER LOVERS KNOW, TIMING IS EVERYTHING.

these buildings—like the later generation of White Towers—reflected the streamlined modern styling that was coming into its own. Krystal also specialized in little square hamburgers that sold for a nickel. Their motto, yet another variation on a familiar theme: "Take along a sack full." Two hundred and fifty Krystals still exist.

Early in the 1930s a small chain of hamburger joints called White Manna flourished in northern New Jersey. The original was conceived as a prime example of the popular prefabricated diner architecture of the day, and was exhibited at the 1939 World's Fair in New York. It was later moved to Jersey City and is operating to this day, not far from its sister Manna—the crown jewel of Hackensack, which still serves the precious little steamy, onion-spiced burgers. The kind even Walt Anderson would be proud of.

Kewpee Hotel Hamburgs, or "Kewpees" as their devoted patrons prefer to call them, was—in its prime—a chain of nearly two hundred powerfully popular Midwestern hamburger stands founded in Flint, Michigan, in the mid-Twenties. Less than ten remain today.

A SHOWPIECE FROM THE 1939 WORLD'S FAIR, THE WHITE MANNA, STILL STANDING IN JERSEY CITY, NEW JERSEY, 1992.

In Lima, Ohio (where there are three), one resident remembers a time in the late Forties when the automotive gridlock in Kewpee's parking lot became such a nightmare that "they installed an automatic turntable in the pavement so the cars could turn around."

In addition to the medieval motifs, another popular architectural style can best be described as the "cozy cottage concept."

In 1927 in Houston the Toddle Houses began as a chain of twelve restaurants (each with a maximum seating capacity of eleven). They were quaintly traditional in style with dual chimneys and white picket fences. These movable structures were said to "toddle" from side to side while being transported by truck from one location to the next. The same year in Louisville, Little Tavern restaurants (still a common sight in Washington, D.C., and Maryland) were designed as friendly cottage buildings with steep, green shingled roofs and the familiar glistening white porcelain enamel interiors. Hamburgers were the main event on the menus of both establishments. Little Tavern Shops (sixteen remain) purveyed a delicious version of the onion-steamed "castle-inspired" miniburger. The Toddle Houses are long gone, but they were known for their burgers "with" (onions), and an innovation known as an "automatic cashier," which was devised to allow the customer to pay his own bill and thus speed up service.

One of America's most popular comic strips of the 1930s featured Popeye the Sailor, and

THE WHITE DIAMOND IN CLARK, NEW JERSEY, AS PRESERVED BY JOHN BAEDER IN HIS 1981 PAINTING.

"KEWPEE HOTEL'S HAMBURGS," PHOTOGRAPHED IN TOLEDO, OHIO,
IN 1974. ONCE A CHAIN OF NEARLY TWO HUNDRED IN THE MIDWEST,
KEWPEE'S MASCOT (RIGHT) HELPED SPREAD THE GOOD WORD.

"the glorified hamburger"

INTERNATIONALLY FAMOUS

IN THE U.S., WIMPY GRILLS SUCCESS-
FULLY TOUTED THEIR "GLORIFIED
HAMBURGER" FOR TWO DECADES, BE-
FORE GOING GLOBAL IN 1954.

a rotund whiskered character named J. Wellington Wimpy whose self-stated raison d'etre was an unrelenting quest for "the acme of ground bovinity." "I would gladly pay you Tuesday for a hamburger today" were the words he lived by. By 1934, the amusing exploits of the world's first burger addict were so familiar to most Americans that, increasingly, hamburgers were referred to as "Wimpy Burgers." That year Wimpy Grills opened as a six-stool hamburger stand in Bloomington, Indiana. The first of a string of hamburger havens that prospered by capitalizing on America's emerging national pastime, and by borrowing (and eventually paying for) the famous Wimpy name.

Incorporating gabled cottage exteriors and the same principle of standardized service as its predecessors, "Wimpys" took a different approach with "The Glorified Hamburger," a radical departure that was priced at twice the norm—a whopping 10 cents! As an upscale, meatier alternative to the pervasively popular nickel version, the glorified hamburger found a niche. By 1954 Wimpy Grills had sold their seventy-five millionth burger, and were operating in Boston, Providence, Chicago, Los Angeles, and throughout Indiana.

The same year, plans were announced to bring the glorious Wimpys to Europe. Five years later, with restaurants established in England, Scotland, Ireland, and Wales, a press release from the home office announced that "the Glorified Hamburger was introduced to consular officials of eighteen more nations at a special occasion in Chicago's Ambassador Hotel where hamburgers on flaming swords and cheeseburgers under glass were featured." In 1977 there were 1,500 Wimpys overseas in 39 countries.

Remembered almost as much for his antisocial behavior as for the glory of his burgers, Wimpy founder Ed Gold had divested himself of all European rights early on (a move which no doubt contributed to his crotchety behavior later in life). Once, when asked what would happen to the business after he died, he barked: "I never got married. And I don't give a goddamn what happens to the business. When I'm six feet under, what the hell difference will it be to me?" A few months later, in 1978, Ed died while tending to burger business in one of his Chicago eateries, and shortly thereafter, on North American soil, all Wimpy Grills were put to rest with their cantankerous founder, who had stipulated in his final will and testament that on his passing, all restaurants were to be closed permanently, and that the Glorified Hamburger be retired . . . *Forever.*

The famous "Bun N' Burger of 34th Street" is a small chain that has been making a lot of people happy in the New York metropolitan area since 1939. That year, the first Bun N' Burger was established on East 34th Street in Manhattan. In its heyday, Bun N' Burger was a thriving system of twenty-two East Coast restaurants. Like many of the hamburger chains that spread infectiously across America in the Thirties and Forties, riding on the coattails of the great White Castle, Bun N' Burger prospered for several decades by recognizing, and catering to, one of America's most basic needs: fast, wholesome, made-to-

order hamburgers. But changes in social patterns, the rise and fall of neighborhoods, along with the increased cost of food and labor, would take their toll.

Although the legendary White Castle endures today by sticking to the basics—a limited, tried-and-true menu built around belly bombers and precious little else—it has also remained competitive by adapting to trends that dictated larger restaurants and less ornate (some would say dated) exterior façades.

Sadly, White Tower and the other 5 cent hamburger chains that mimicked Walt Anderson and Billy Ingram's recipe for success would find it increasingly difficult to do business into the Sixties and Seventies, as an emerging generation of national hamburger chains would take fast food to the legal limit, offering prepackaged, high-speed hamburgers and the irresistible lure of instantaneous burger gratification.

WHITE TOWER BURGERS WERE STILL FABULOUS IN THE FIFTIES, AS THIS SATISFIED CUSTOMER'S DELIGHTED EXPRESSION ATTESTS.

DRIVE-IN DREAMS

LIFE IN THE FAST LANE

By the 1920s Americans were proud owners of nearly nine million automobiles. Roadside eateries now competed for the business of these motorists with distinctive architecture designed to command attention. Initially these restaurants were a mixed bag of architectural oddities including buildings shaped like root-beer barrels, chili bowls, and four-legged animals.

Drugstore soda fountains were known to have served refreshments to customers remaining in their buggies, but the Pig Stand on the Dallas-Fort Worth Highway is considered the first roadside restaurant specifically designed for automotive dining.

The dream began in Dallas in 1921 when J. O. Kirby observed that "people with cars are so lazy that they don't want to get out of them to eat." Shortly thereafter, he opened his first Pig Stand and began dispensing sandwiches to patrons in their cars.

AMERICAS FIRST DRIVE-IN WAS THE PIG STAND, FOUNDED IN DALLAS IN 1921. THE TWENTY-THIRD UNIT WENT UP IN LOS ANGELES ABOUT 1927. IN 1936, ARCHITECT WAYNE MC-ALLISTER UNVEILED HERBERT'S, AT THE CORNER OF BEVERLY AND FAIRFAX IN LOS ANGELES (TOP).

EARLY ROADSIDE EATERIES OFTEN USED ODD-SHAPED BUILDINGS TO REACH OUT TO MOTORISTS. "SIZE," A CALIFORNIA COLLOQUIALISM FOR "HAMBURGER WITH CHILI," WAS A FEATURED ATTRACTION AT THE CHILI BOWL.

HAMBURGER MAN STANLEY BURKE FOUNDED HIS SUCCESSFUL CHAIN OF STAN'S DRIVE-INS IN SACRAMENTO IN 1934

THE GRANDEST AND MOST GLORIOUS DRIVE-INS WERE ONCE FOUND IN LOS ANGELES. IN THE 1930S, CARPENTER'S, AT WILSHIRE AND FAIRFAX, AND SIMON'S, ON PICO BOULEVARD, EPITOMIZED THE GENRE.

By the 1930s there were thirty Drive-in Pig Stands serving barbecue (and burgers) across the nation.

The drive-in may have originated in Texas, but it was in California, in the 1930s and '40s, that it evolved. California classics include Mel's, Stan's, Carpenter's, Simon's, Delores's and Tiny Naylor's. Their bold lighting and strikingly modern design reflected the streamlined styling of the aerodynamic autos whizzing by. Circular neon-adorned structures offered 360-degree parking and "a real Hamburger sandwich" for 15 cents.

The Steak 'n Shake drive-in chain, founded in Normal, Illinois, in 1934, helped drive-ins spread east. It compensated for limitations imposed by cold weather by offering indoor dining and aggressive pro-

ELECTRONIC ORDERING DEVICES PROMPTED SONIC DRIVE-IN'S PLEDGE TO DELIVER "SERVICE WITH THE SPEED OF SOUND."

HOW TO USE
TELETRAY®

1.—Push Button on Microspeaker.
2.— Wait for operator who will ask for your order.
3.— Give order — relax and enjoy fast service and fine food.
4.—Re-orders filled Promptly.

motions of their carryout service. In the 1990s Steak 'n Shake continued to be "famous for steakburgers" at 120 restaurants in the Midwest and Southeast, although they dispensed with carhop service in the 1970s.

The early drive-ins hired young boys to deliver orders on hanging window trays. Speed was the name of the game and these "tray boys" would run up to the cars the moment they pulled in, hopping up to the running board before the car had reached a full stop—thus the name "carhop." By the 1950s the carhop's responsibilities were reduced by half when many drive-ins installed high-tech electronic ordering devices with names like Electro-Hop, Teletray, and Fone-A-Chef. It was no longer necessary for a hop to take the order, just deliver it.

MODERN TECHNOLOGY CAN BE FUN! TELETRAY, ELECTRO-HOP, AND FONE-A-CHEF WERE AMONG SCORES OF AUTOMATIC ORDERING SYSTEMS THAT BECAME THE RAGE IN THE FIFTIES.

IN THE EAST AND MIDWEST, RICHARD'S PROMOTED "CAR-FETERIA" SERVICE. THIS 1957 PHOTOGRAPH SHOWS A DRIVE-IN IN CAMBRIDGE, MASSACHUSETTS.

In Shawnee, Oklahoma, in 1959, Troy Smith started the chain of Sonic drive-ins whose slogan "service at the speed of sound" was inspired by this space-age gadgetry. For decades Sonic bucked the trend for self-service and it survived, remarkably, into the 1990s to become America's largest chain of drive-ins, and the fifth-largest hamburger chain, while continuing to offer carhop service.

In their heyday drive-ins were considered a respectable place for the family, but by the Fifties they were increasingly becoming teenage territory—

EVERETT WILLIAMS OPERATED HIS ANN ARBOR DRIVE-IN FOR TWENTY-FOUR YEARS BEFORE TAKING A NASTY SPILL ON THE ICE ONE NIGHT WHILE DELIVERING THIRTEEN CALIFORNIA BURGERS TO FRIENDS. THE HIP INJURY WHICH RESULTED FORCED HIS EARLY RETIREMENT, BUT IN 1992, TO THE DELIGHT OF THE LOCAL POPULATION, HE RETURNED TO THE BURGER BUSINESS.

CALIFORNIA CRUISING AT MEL'S DRIVE-IN WAS IMMORTAL-
IZED BY ARTIST PETER PALOMBI, IN HIS 1972 ILLUSTRATION.

IN THE 1960S, STATE-OF-THE-ART DRIVE-INS PROTECTED
THEIR CARHOPS AND BURGERS FROM THE ELEMENTS WITH
STYLIZED CANOPIES IN FESTIVE SHAPES AND COLORS.

havens for the high school set in search of action. Often several of these burger palaces were located on the same strip where a steady stream of teenagers in cars would "cruise for burgers." But more time was actually spent loitering and looking for a date than laying down money on burgers.

By the late Sixties, problems with rowdy teenagers, drugs, alcohol, and vandalism had eroded the once regal reputation of the drive-in, and led to its impending demise. As communities nationwide instituted local ordinances in an attempt to keep noise and litter under control, and rising real estate costs were cutting into profits, an ambitious program of national highway construction signaled the inevitable end of the era. Traffic was rerouted, bypassing the commercial strip and denying multitudes of motorists access to the local burgers.

ARCHITECT DOUGLAS HONNALD'S
SLEEK 1949 JETSTREAM DESIGN
FOR TINY NAYLOR'S IN HOLLYWOOD.
ON OPENING NIGHT HUMPHREY
BOGART DESCRIBED IT AS A "HUGE
BIRD ABOUT TO TAKE OFF."

RANCHBURGERS WERE THE SPECIALTY OF BOB COLGLAZIER'S RANCH HOUSE DRIVE-INS IN INDIANA AND KENTUCKY.

STEAK 'N SHAKE DRIVE-INS
HAVE BEEN "FAMOUS FOR
STEAKBURGERS" SINCE THEY
FIRST URGED PATRONS TO
"TAKHOMASAK" IN THE 1930S.

HAMBURGER HELPERS

THE DIVAS OF DELUXE

AT THE LOCAL DRIVE-IN, BURGER-BEARING DREAM-GIRLS SUCH AS BRENDA HELPED PUT THE AMOUR IN GLAMOUR, AND THE KITSCH IN THE KITCHEN.

Where would the hamburger be today without its handmaidens? The burger has traditionally relied upon a delightful array of colorful and charismatic hamburger handlers to deliver the goods. From the beginning, there has been a special relationship between the grateful burger consumer and the gracious patty purveyor.

In the early 1900s when Upton Sinclair's *The Jungle* exposed unsavory practices within Chicago's meat-packing industry, people grew apprehensive about what might be going through the meat grinder, and the image of the hamburger suffered. America's first hamburger eatery chain, White Castle, recognized the need to reassure a concerned public, and went to great lengths to spread the good word.

In 1932, they created Julia Joyce, a fictional in-house hamburger spokeswoman. Julia was miraculously present at every White Castle. It was her mission to infiltrate local women's club functions armed with bags of free burgers. Warm, witty, and vivacious, Julia charmed the ladies who lunched, allaying any fears they may have had with regard to the nutritional qualifications of the product.

Prior to World War II, both White Castle

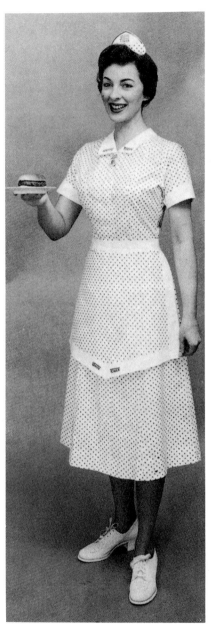

WHITE TOWER'S STYLISH YET UNDER-
STATED TOWERETTES AIMED TO
PLEASE. THEIR WARDROBE MAY HAVE
CHANGED SUBTLY WITH THE TIMES, BUT
THE SMILES REMAINED THE SAME.

SERVICE WITH A STYLE!

and White Tower employed male counter help exclusively, and hopping cars was a manly vocation. During the war, however, women moved in to fill the ranks, and they never left. At White Tower, the Towerettes were a legion of waitresses dressed like nurses on a mercy mission and possessed with the spirit of Radio City Rockettes.

At the nation's drive-ins tray boys were replaced by attractive young girls with perky personalities and "come hither" smiles. Job qualifications often included good figures and spic and span appearances. Some drive-ins even instituted personal grooming training programs, and most enforced strict appearance guidelines. One business's list of dos and don'ts instructed carhops to "Remember, a lot of eyes are upon you! Keep your nose powdered, lipstick on straight, and hair combed," but warned against eye shadow, heavily painted fingernails, and "chewing gum with abandon."

Many drive-ins adopted distinctive uniforms for their tray girls to enhance the favorable impression on customers. By the mid-1950s these female carhops had become the reigning queens of the drive-in scene.

BOB'S CALIFORNIA BIG BOY (TOP) AND HOUSTON'S BRONCO DRIVE-INS BEDECKED THEIR HOPS IN THE LATEST STYLES FOR HAMBURGER HANDLERS.

THE RANCH HOUSE IN LOUISVILLE OPTED
FOR THE MAJORETTE MOTIF.

© MCA Records

ROLLER-SKATING ATTENDANTS MAY HAVE STARTED WITH THE GAS STATIONS OF THE
THIRTIES, BUT DAVID WILLARDSON'S ILLUSTRATION FOR THE 1972 FILM *AMERI-
CAN GRAFFITI* REMINDS US WHERE THEY WERE PUT TO THEIR GREATEST USE.

A BIG BOY IS BORN

BOB WIAN DOUBLES THE FUN

THE ORIGINAL BIG BOY.

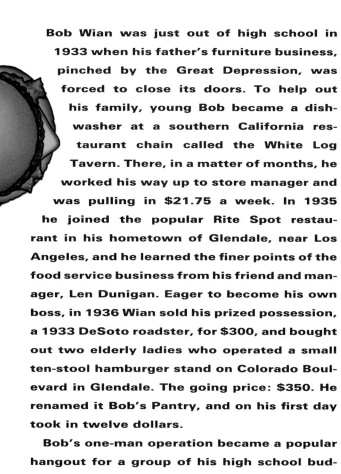

Bob Wian was just out of high school in 1933 when his father's furniture business, pinched by the Great Depression, was forced to close its doors. To help out his family, young Bob became a dishwasher at a southern California restaurant chain called the White Log Tavern. There, in a matter of months, he worked his way up to store manager and was pulling in $21.75 a week. In 1935 he joined the popular Rite Spot restaurant in his hometown of Glendale, near Los Angeles, and he learned the finer points of the food service business from his friend and manager, Len Dunigan. Eager to become his own boss, in 1936 Wian sold his prized possession, a 1933 DeSoto roadster, for $300, and bought out two elderly ladies who operated a small ten-stool hamburger stand on Colorado Boulevard in Glendale. The going price: $350. He renamed it Bob's Pantry, and on his first day took in twelve dollars.

Bob's one-man operation became a popular hangout for a group of his high school buddies, members of Chuck Foster's Orchestra, who would often stop in for a late night bite after a gig. Bob always knew what they wanted. Naturally they'd order hamburgers . . . and lots of 'em. One chilly February night in 1937, Stewie Strange, the bass player, was heard to utter these words: "How 'bout

THE LEGENDARY BOB WIAN, INVENTOR OF THE DOUBLE-DECKER HAMBURGER, BEHIND THE COUNTER OF HIS FIRST BOB'S IN 1937.

something different for a change, Bob?'' Wian decided to have a little fun with the guy. He carved a sesame seed bun in three slices, added two burgers between them, then layered it with lettuce, cheese, and relish.

Mr. Wian maintains that it was his intention to make this leaning tower of burger ''look ridiculous'' and thereby fill his customer's request for something truly ''different.'' But, as he tells it, ''the double-deck burger juices were absorbed by the center bun. It was delicious, and everybody in the band wanted one.'' At that moment, yet another major milestone in the course of hamburger evolution,

Bob's BIG BOY HAMBURGER

Made as Only We Know How...
Two Patties of Freshly Ground
Hamburger, Served on a
Special Baked Sesame Seed
Toasted Bun with Mayon-
naise, Lettuce, Cheese
and Topped with Our
Own Relish . . . .

45¢

Bob knew that he was onto something—this fistful of fun on a bun—ought to have a name.

The name came almost as quickly as the concept, and was inspired by a chunk of a lad named Richard Woodruff, who would often drop by the Pantry to help Bob out with sweeping and cleaning chores in exchange for a hamburger or two. Richard was six, and lived down the street. He was short, plump, and as the story goes, he would often wander into the restaurant wearing a pair of droopy overalls. His nickname was "Fat Boy," a name Wian initially considered for his bigger, better burger, but "Fat Boy" was already in use as a product trademark, so he christened his creation the "Big Boy" hamburger. Another regular at the Pantry, a Hollywood cartoonist, sketched the now famous "Big Boy" caricature on a napkin, an image which launched several billion burger bites.

When word got around about Bob's invention, folks began to line up for a taste, and as sales of the Big Boy sandwich sizzled, other burgermeisters took note. Soon double-decker burgers were as common as bunk beds at summer camp, and rotund little "Burger Boy" mascots were everywhere, as Big

AS HIS FAME GREW, THE BIG BOY EVOLVED, AND SCORES OF IMITATORS LIKE GOODY BOY AND FAT BOY FOLLOWED HIS LEAD.

48

Boy begat Chubby Boy, Hi-Boy, Bun Boy, Beefy Boy, Country Boy, Brawny Boy, Husky Boy, Yumy Boy, Lucky Boy, Super Boy, and several hundred other variations on the theme.

Within three years, Bob had enlarged his original location and opened a second in the Los Angeles area. In 1948 the king of the double-decker hamburger was voted mayor of Glendale. By 1949 he was the proud father of three Big Boy Restaurants, each combining a modern coffee shop interior with a "snappy service" drive-in in the rear of the building. In 1950 over 2½ million Big Boys were served, and by 1955 his growing chain of burger emporiums sold 5 million 45-cent Big Boys, on which his staff of burger builders (affectionately referred to as "Boyfriends") applied 38,000 gallons of mayonnaise, 5 million bottles of ketchup, and 25,000 gallons of relish.

By the mid-Forties Wian started looking eastward. In 1946 he signed a franchising agreement with Dave Frish of Frish's restaurants in Cincinnati, paving the way for Frish's Big Boys to enter Ohio, Kentucky, Indiana, and Florida. In franchising the Big Boy name regionally the unique arrangement allowed each particular sponsor to claim the Big Boy as its own. Hence the variety of independent surnames attached to the famous Big Boy burger: In Michigan the hamburger was marketed at Elias Brothers' Big Boy Restaurants. In Tennessee it was the exclusive property of Shoney's, and of Kip's in Texas, Oklahoma, and Kansas. It was Manner's Big Boy in Cleveland, Vip's in New Mexico, Abdow's in Massachusetts, J.B's in Utah and Nevada, while Elby's brought the Big Boy to Pennsylvania and West Virginia.

WIAN'S FIRST BIG BOY RESTAURANT, BOB'S PANTRY, ON COLORADO BOULEVARD IN GLENDALE, CALIFORNIA.

IN THE MID-SIXTIES, FRISCH'S BIG BOY BROUGHT THE FLAMBOYANT CALIFORNIA-STYLE COFFEE SHOP DESIGNS OF ARMET AND DAVIS TO TAMPA, FLORIDA.

HOME OF FAMOUS "ROYAL BOY" STEAKBURGERS

In Phoenix in 1956, amid considerable fanfare, Bob unveiled "the nation's most elaborate hamburger joint." At a cost of over a half a million dollars, the newest home of the Big Boy drew crowds in record numbers. *Time* reported "a dawn to dusk flow of people and automobiles drawn by a compelling image: the 12-foot-high statue of a bright-eyed, chubby child, with a brown cowlick, and 'Big Boy' emblazoned on his chest."

This state-of-the-art operation, described in restaurant trade journals as "a drive-in coffee shop," provided drive-in service for fifty cars, and a large dining room with counter service seating one hundred. The design included two kitchens and dual fountains, better to serve the restaurant's split personality, and enough

COUNTRY BOY

BU BOY

Googies

equipment for "grinding and molding hamburger patties by the thousands."

A few weeks after the Phoenix debut, Bob announced plans to modernize and expand coffee shop service at two of his existing Big Boy outlets, and to open two new ambitious establishments that year in the hamburger hungry San Fernando Valley. By the end of the year, he was keeping extremely busy with thirteen drive-in coffee shops, and was overheard saying something about an early retirement.

The man who made quite a name (and a fortune) for himself by inventing the double-decker hamburger was quick to recognize a burger bonanza in coffee shops. Bob built his last drive-in in 1964, and focused on the "family style" coffee shops which would continue to feed his good fortune for decades. In the Fabulous Fifties' final hour, a fantastic new roadside vernacular was taking (unusual) shape in California.

The infamous Googies landed in Hollywood in 1949. From the moment Googies opened its doors on Sunset Boulevard, people took notice. They had no choice. As designed by architect John Laughtner, this building flaunted an abstract profile whose unlikely mixture of shapes and materials represented an offbeat, energetic modernism that was to become an architectural metaphor for the genre.

Googies' critics attacked it for its "unre-

ON SUNSET BOULEVARD IN LOS ANGELES, GOOGIES COFFEE SHOP WAS PRACTICALLY STOPPING TRAFFIC IN 1949—AND THAT WAS THE WHOLE IDEA.

IN 1951, THE CLOCK WAS ARMET AND DAVIS'S FIRST COFFEE SHOP DESIGN. IT WAS ALSO THE HOME OF A FEISTY BURGER NAMED CHUBBY THE CHAMP.

DUTCH TWINBURGERS

BURGER BOY

CLOCK

TWICE AS BIG   TWICE AS GOOD

A BEACON FOR BURGER EATERS SINCE 1956, AT LA CIENEGA AND OLYMPIC BOULEVARD, LOS ANGELES.

strained excesses,'' dismissing it as a gimmicky attention-getter . . . which it was. A flamboyant and futuristic vision to the approaching motorist, Googies' most distinctive feature was its red steel horizontal roofline which, when you least expected it, took a sudden turn for the sky, and ended abruptly as a vertical signboard displaying Googies' trademark—a cartoon moniker design, with bulging ''goo-goo eyes.''

In spite of its critics, Googies prospered. Other restaurant owners took note and soon followed suit, with equally adventurous exterior motifs whose exaggerated rooflines and angles infused a new sense of exhilaration into the roadside vernacular. As a symbol of

free exploration of modern form and shape, Googies would become synonymous with the daring and flamboyant visual wildness which characterized the architectural style of the California coffee shop. Googies was also known for its excellent hamburgers, ground fresh and pattied daily.

Although Laughtner's previous work for Coffee Dan's Restaurants in Los Angeles in the early Forties is credited with initiating the architectural genre, he found himself repeatedly defending his Googies design to stuffy critics who considered the style excessive and haphazard. But as influential and effective as Googies proved to be, Laughtner had apparently had enough of the coffee shop business,

BIFF'S TINY COFFEE SHOPS, AS DESIGNED BY DOUGLAS HONNALD, WERE STRIKING AND STYLISH. THEIR CHEF OFFERS COMFORT FOOD.

and went on to other ventures. The Los Angeles firm of Louis Armet and Eldon Davis would carry the torch for coffee shop modernism, succeeding brilliantly where John Laughtner left off.

The California coffee shops had a whole lot going for them. In addition to their powerful visual imagery, and comfortable friendly environment, many were open twenty-four hours providing hamburgers throughout the night (and even combination egg and burger breakfasts). Round the clock burgers! A welcome addition to the roadside strip. When Armet and Davis designed a second and a third building utilizing the stylized signature roof, *American Restaurant* took note in a banner headline: "Eyecatching Roofs Catch More Business." The article reported that "Beautiful and business-compelling roofs are a cornerstone of the architects' design philosophy." Their work went on to include such classic southern California coffee and burger emporiums as Bob's Big Boy, Norms, Ships, Panns, Denny's, Penguin's, The Clock, and The Huddle.

Although some of the California coffee shops would continue to offer curb service well into the Sixties, the emphasis was increasingly on interior dining. The spacious Armet and Davis interiors were as stimulating as the exteriors, with dramatic angles and curves dashing off in all directions, sparkling walls of windows, vibrant color schemes, suspended light fixtures designed for the space age, and modern seating by cutting edge designers such as Charles Eames. An energized atmosphere all the better for eating burgers.

Martin Cable owned and operated Corky's coffee shop in Sherman Oaks, California, which he purchased from Stan (the drive-in man) in 1962. By the time he sold the business thirty years later, it was the largest volume coffee shop operating in Los Angeles. Martin never sold a hamburger that he didn't make

that day. "At Corky's we went through five chucks a day. That's between 500 and 600 pounds of beef, or roughly 7000 hamburgers daily. We were open 24 hours, and we had 8 different burgers on the menu. Hamburgers were always the best sellers." The ultimate example of Coffee Shop Modern was Ships. Three were built in the late Fifties in and around Los Angeles, two still remain. Author Alan Hess describes the thrill of the Ships experience: "It's as if all these modernistic shapes were collected in some wondrous new force field to shelter modern man at the corner of Glendon and Wilshire." Ships' dynamic sign—glowing free-form letters encased in circular neon and pierced by a stylized boomerang angled radiantly toward the outer limits—still is very George Jetson.

At Ships they are proud of their sign, and their hamburgers. And just in case there are any doubts, they've included their "five points to wholesome hamburger" on the back of the menu. They grind it daily in their own kitchen,

PANN'S COFFEE SHOP IS A SURVIVOR FROM 1956. AN OASIS OF GOOD TIMES ON LA CIENEGA BOULEVARD IN LOS ANGELES.

THE CLOVERFIELD HUDDLE
FEATURED DELICIOUS
HUDDLE-BURGERS IN 1955.
THE PENGUIN (BELOW),
FOUNDED IN SANTA MONICA
IN 1959, WAS SERVING
THREE-POUND MONSTER
BURGERS UNTIL ITS UN-
TIMELY DEMISE IN 1991.

and take pride in claiming that "it is impossible to improve upon the cleanliness of preparing our ground meat or to improve upon its delicious flavor. Eaters can eat them raw if they so desire. Please try yours rare." Knowing full well that a good coffee shop was often judged by the quality of its burgers, all modern coffee shops paid special attention to these sacred sandwiches on their menus. Most offered house special burgers. At Ships, the out of this world Ship-shape Burger sold better than the hotcakes.

Biff's, one of the first and most widely imitated of the southern California chains, was owned by Tiny Naylor's son Biff. The Hollywood location was designed by Douglas Honnald, and built on the principle of a lean-to. Biff's sign featured a grinning, wide-eyed chef with a steaming hamburger platter in hand. The famous Biff-Burger was served open face. It too had been freshly ground, and had nothing whatsoever to hide.

In 1956, there were four popular Huddle restaurants in Los Angeles and Santa Monica. That year the location on Wilshire Boulevard was said to tab the highest twenty-four-hour auto traffic in the western United States, and in May they celebrated the sale of their one millionth Huddle-burger. The Huddle-burger is described in the menu as "delicious in any language. Created for a big appetite, the Huddle-burger is loaded with one-half pound of U.S. choice beef, ground fresh daily in our kitchen and served on a protein-rich bun, with melted cheese, red-ripe tomato, onion slice, crisp lettuce, pickles and our own relish. Try one now, then tell your friends."

By the mid-Sixties, the modern spirit of Coffee Shop Modern was enthusiastically embraced from coast to coast. Big Boy restaurants designed by Armet and Davis brought the exuberant and impulsive aesthetic to Indiana, Ohio, and Florida. In the Chicago area, a regional chain of Peter Pan coffee

BOB'S GARDEN GROVE, 1957, WAS THE FIRST DESIGNED BY ARMET AND DAVIS. BALLOTS PROPOSED AN END TO THE BIG BOY IN 1985 (LEFT).

shops incorporated the boisterous style with a menu built around Dagwood Burgers, Olive Burgers, and "America's Number One Hamburger Treat"—The Peter Pan Burger.

As the energized decade raced to an end, the national mood began to move away from the free-spirited optimism of the Fifties. Futuristic imagery and design were increasingly abandoned in favor of a more toned down approach. The heyday of Googie coffee and burger emporiums was coming to a close.

Bob Wian continued to expand his Big Boy empire. As the world's first hamburger franchise mogul, he ironically set the stage for a national 15-cent hamburger franchising epidemic, which would ultimately draw legions of burger lovers away from the drive-ins and coffee shops and into the swift and thrifty world of the self-service hamburger stand.

In 1967 Wian sold his booming Big Boy enterprise to the Marriott Corporation, which adapted the outlets to the current taste for more subtle surroundings. In some parts of the country, the legendary Big Boy hamburger underwent some subtle modifications as well. In California, angry lifetime Bob's aficionados accused the new owners of scrimping on the family recipe. Later, when Marriott decided to

strengthen its profile as a "family restaurant," they came to the conclusion that the Big Boy should no longer be seen with a hamburger platter in his hand. Tony Gutierrez was hired to do the dirty work. In California he meticulously severed the burger-bearing arms off hundreds of Big Boy statues, fitting new limbs whose outstretched reach culminated anticlimactically in an empty-handed wave. "It was rather traumatic," he recalled later. "I grew up on Big Boys. I hated to see his hamburgers go."

Adding insult to injury, in 1985 Marriott seriously considered doing away with the Big Boy character. After a national referendum—it was determined that he would be allowed to stay on a while longer (albeit burgerless).

But his days did appear to be numbered, at least in California. In 1992, Marriott sold every last Bob's Big Boy to an investment group, for $65 million. It was immediately announced that all 120 units would be converted to "Cocos or Carrows family dining concepts."

Meanwhile in Michigan, the Elias brothers franchise acquired the Big Boy trademark and franchising rights from Marriott, with the expressed intention of "keeping the familiar icon around for some time." The rotund one is, after all, an American institution.

IN THE FIFTIES, CHICAGOANS WERE CRAZY ABOUT PETER PAN'S BURGERS.

A BIG BURGER BOOM

THE FIFTEEN CENT PHENOMENON

In the summer of 1928, Richard McDonald left his native New Hampshire and joined his brother Maurice in Hollywood, where they worked as truck drivers for Columbia Studios. It was the Depression, and, as Richard remembers, their father lost his job of forty-two years with the simple line: "You've outlived your usefulness." Devastated, the brothers vowed to become financially independent. It was their dream to own a chain of movie theaters.

Within a few years they had put enough money aside to purchase a small movie house in Glendora, just east of Los Angeles. They renamed it the Beacon Theater, and adopted the sales pitch: "Let the Beacon light guide you to better entertainment." But times were lean, and the crowds just weren't coming. The brothers did notice that Walt Wiley's little hot dog stand nearby was doing a brisk business. And they also discovered a Sunkist orange packing plant, where all oranges that had fallen to the ground before being picked were discarded. In a juicy deal, "Mac" and Richard made arrangements with the plant supervisor to purchase the fallen fruit—twenty dozen for a quarter, and in 1937, opened their own drive-in (featuring fresh O.J. and hot dogs), near a racetrack in Arcadia. Soon they discovered that Californians preferred hamburgers to hot dogs, and adapted their menu accordingly.

MAURICE AND RICHARD MCDONALD OUTSIDE THEIR REVOLUTIONARY NEW "HAMBURGER BAR" IN SAN BERNARDINO PRIOR TO ITS OPENING IN 1948.

MCDONALD'S NEW "CUSTOM-BUILT" BURGERS WERE CHAMPIONED ON THIS 1950S BAG BY A NEW HAMBURGER-HEADED MASCOT NAMED SPEEDY.

LET'S EAT OUT!, PUBLISHED IN 1965, DETAILED THE ADVENTURES OF TOM AND SUE, WHO WERE GIVEN A GRAND TOUR AND A MARVELOUS MEAL AT THEIR LOCAL MCDONALD'S.

For the next three years, the brothers learned the food service business, while realizing modest profits. In 1940, they cut their octagonal building in half and transported it to a busy thoroughfare near a high school in San Bernardino, enlarged the building to accommodate more customers, and added twenty carhops. Hamburgers were 35 cents.

For seven years they worked day and night. Mac had the day shift, Richard the evening hours. The operation became the most popular hangout in town. By 1948, although quite comfortable financially, the McDonalds were growing restless. They closed the carhop service drive-in. "We were bored, and we wanted to try something different" explained Richard. "Ninety percent of our business was hamburgers, and we wondered what would happen if we sold almost nothing else but hamburgers, cut the price to 15 cents, eliminated carhop service, reduced the staff from about fifty to five, got rid of plates, forks, knives, and tipping, and just made the whole thing a cheap, efficient operation where people wouldn't have to wait." Richard had always considered it "damned inefficient and discourteous to keep someone waiting." Especially for burgers.

What a concept! They would call it "McDonald's New Self-Service System." No cute and cuddly hamburger handlers, no dishwashers, no waiting, and a streamlined burger-based menu. The burgers would be smaller (10 to a pound instead of 8), cheaper (less than half the 35-cent price), prepackaged, and pre-dressed with no choice in applied condiments. The 15-cent McDonald's hamburger would come with ketchup, pickle, and onion only. They would be called "customized hamburgers" but, in fact, the customer had no choice in the matter. Allowing customers to personalize their burgers would slow the whole operation down. The drive-in closed for alterations, and a billboard appeared out front informing the confused and the curious that "America's first drive-in hamburger bar would be opening soon." At the heart of this revolutionary concept was a fantastic idea: *Faster Burgers For All.*

When the new operation opened on December 20, 1948, confusion reigned. Customers would park their cars in the lot, honk, and wait for a carhop that never came. Angry patrons, unwilling to serve themselves (and not too thrilled about the idea of disposing of their own trash) were not quick to recognize the advantages of this bold new experiment.

Eventually, as word got around about the exceptionally fast, bargain-priced burgers, people were won over. Seven months later, customers were lining up outside the walk-up service window in droves. The crush of people was so severe (lines formed of over two hundred) that the brothers devised a means of cooking their burgers and fries ahead and keeping them warm under infrared lamps. They were the first to utilize the lamps for this purpose.

The McDonalds' operation was becoming as famous for its 10-cent french fries as its hamburgers. Neither were frozen in those days, and Richard recalls: "Whenever anyone came to us and tried to sell us something frozen we'd say, 'No way!' " In the relentless pursuit of potato perfection, he and Mac researched "the perfect fry," determined that the secret lay in proper aging. They even built a special potato-aging warehouse in San Bernardino.

Word of this radical new approach to hamburger cookery traveled fast. Soon the astounding popularity of the new self-service drive-in was the talk of the food service industry. *American Restaurant* magazine visited the San Bernardino hamburger stand and reported in a cover story that "McDonald's entire system is based on speed. Forty hamburgers are turned out in 110 seconds on a specially built polished steel griddle." Dis-

THE FIRST SELF-SERVICE MCDONALD'S WAS AN OCTAGONAL STRUCTURE ON E STREET IN SAN BERNARDINO.

pensers were developed for ketchup and mustard that, with a thumb control, "efficiently provide an exact, controlled amount of these condiments on each bun."

The world's first hamburger bar attracted laborers, teenagers, and families alike. In 1951 McDonald's sold $275,000 worth of burgers, shakes, and fries, serving over one million burgers. Four years and six million hamburgers after their disastrous opening, the brothers announced ambitious new plans to expand the self-service concept to a national system of franchised restaurants.

They decided to establish a more distinctive look to their revolutionary hamburger stand. The original octagonal building had been inspired by other successful drive-ins in Los Angeles such as Carpenter's and Simon's, but

ANOTHER MCDONALD INNOVATION TO SPEED SERVICE: A CUSTOMIZED KETCHUP DISPENSER WITH SINGLE-HANDED "THUMB-CONTROL."

The Most Important 60 Seconds in Your Entire Life!

YES — THE NEXT 60 SECONDS MAY ALTER THE COURSE OF YOUR ENTIRE LIFE!

YOU ARE LOOKING AT A PICTURE OF THE NEW "McDONALD SELF SERVICE DRIVE IN"—
THE MOST REVOLUTIONARY DEVELOPMENT IN THE RESTAURANT
INDUSTRY DURING THE PAST 50 YEARS!

IMAGINE—NO CAR HOPS—NO WAITRESSES—NO WAITERS—NO DISHWASHERS—NO BUS BOYS
THE McDONALD SYSTEM IS SELF SERVICE!
NO MORE GLASSWARE—NO MORE DISHES—NO MORE SILVERWARE
THE McDONALD SYSTEM ELIMINATES ALL OF THIS!
IN OUR MODEL DRIVE IN HERE IN SAN BERNARDINO, CALIF., WE SELL MORE THAN A MILLION
HAMBURGERS A YEAR—MORE THAN A HALF MILLION MALTS, SHAKES & SOFT DRINKS A YEAR—
MORE THAN A HALF MILLION ORDERS OF FRENCH FRIES A YEAR!
COMPLETE PLANS ARE NOW AVAILABLE!
WE PROMISED IT WOULD TAKE 60 SECONDS TO READ THIS. THE 60 SECONDS ARE NOW UP.

FOR FURTHER INFORMATION WITHOUT OBLIGATION
WRITE, WIRE OR PHONE
Pats. Pending **McDonald's - Main Office - 1396 "E" St., San Bernardino, Cal.** Pats. Pending

THIS AD IN *AMERICAN RESTAURANT* IN 1952 ANNOUNCES THE MCDONALD BROTHERS' PLANS TO FRANCHISE THEIR SELF-SERVICE SYSTEM. AT THE TIME THEY HAD YET TO FINALIZE THE NEW RESTAURANT DESIGN.

The final outcome was a strikingly original vision of flamboyant modernism—a gleaming red-and-white-tiled building with large canted windows, and parabolic arches of glowing neon. An eye-grabbing sign was also devised for the front of the lot, which repeated the arch motif and featured a mascot named Speedy. Speedy was an animated chef with a hamburger-patty head, a winking eye, and fast feet in motion. The arches were golden during the day, and in the evening came magically to life with flashing pink-and-white neon.

In May 1953, the first McDonald's franchise utilizing the brash new candy-colored design opened in Phoenix, Arizona, and in August the second opened in Downey, California. By the time a milkshake-machine salesman by the name of Ray Kroc got wind of the McDonald's 15-cent burger bonanza, the brothers had sold twenty-one franchises, nine of which were already in operation.

In 1954, after hearing stories of the brothers' remarkably profitable system, Kroc visited the San Bernardino store (which by now was approaching legendary status). He sat in the parking lot and observed firsthand the steady stream of patrons, whose cravings were satisfied within moments at this hamburger oasis in the southern California desert.

Months later, the McDonald's franchise agent retired unexpectedly, and Kroc was given the rights to sell franchises nationally. But the brothers, who preferred to remain close to home, continued to franchise their restaurants in the West.

In 1955, they demolished their original octagonal hamburger bar and replaced it with

now something as bold and modern as their self-serve concept was needed—an eye-catching building that would be distinctly identified as a McDonald's.

With architect Stanley Meston, Richard designed the prototype restaurant; an interior laid out with production line hamburgers in mind. McDonald had a pretty clear vision of what he wanted his new restaurant to be. He sketched a building with a roof that flared dramatically upward in front, giving the illusion of added height. He then added giant arches on either side, thrusting through the roof and spanning the entire length of the building. The architect initially rejected the idea, but the brothers persisted.

RICHARD MCDONALD CAME UP WITH THE IDEA OF THE ARCHES, BUT HAD DIFFICULTY FINDING AN ARCHITECT WHO WAS WILLING TO WORK WITH HIM ON THE DESIGN. "ONE FELLOW ASKED ME IF I HAD A NIGHTMARE PRIOR TO HATCHING THE IDEA," RICHARD RECALLED YEARS LATER.

IN 1973, THIS FRIENDLY SIGHT IN THE NIGHT WAS ON BASCOM AVENUE, IN SAN JOSE. AN ORIGINAL FROM 1964, STILL FUNCTIONING ON 152ND STREET IN CLEVELAND IN 1988 (BELOW).

ARCHIE MCDONALD DID A BRIEF STINT AS THE COMPANY MASCOT FOR SIX MONTHS IN 1964

the new, improved, arched version. The same year, Ray Kroc opened his first McDonald's franchise in Des Plaines, Illinois, and in 1956 he added twelve additional franchises in Illinois, Indiana, and California. Three years later there would be one hundred McDonald's operating nationally—sixty-seven opening in that year alone. In 1961, Kroc bought out the McDonald brothers for $2.7 million in cash.

In Ray Kroc's 1978 biography *Grinding It Out,* he states that he founded the McDonald's Hamburger chain and built it from a single restaurant in Des Plaines, Illinois. This bit of revisionist history really gets Richard's goat. ''Suddenly, after we sold, my golly, he elevated himself to founder! It really burns the hell out of me,'' he told the *Wall Street Journal* in 1991.

Kroc didn't invent McDonald's, but with marketing savvy and astute salesmanship, he transformed it. In the late Fifties he made subtle alterations in the building by rounding out the arches slightly, removing the neon, and fitting them with yellow plastic covers. The spirit of the original Meston/McDonald design remained essentially unchanged, however, until the late Sixties.

The extraordinary success of the McDonald's self-service concept and the radiant structure that housed it were so compellingly original, that they inspired a national 15-cent hamburger craze, and ushered in a new era in hamburger history. Entrepreneurs nationwide rushed to get in on the act, and in the burger

JACK IN THE BOX INTRODUCED THE DRIVE-THRU AND THEIR UNIQUE ROOFTOP TRADEMARK TO SAN DIEGO IN 1951.

SANDY'S WAS ONE OF DOZENS OF HAMBURGER CHAINS TO BORROW THE MCDONALD'S FORMULA.

boom that ensued, a hamburger franchising frenzy spread bargain burgers coast to coast.

Often the imitators borrowed McDonald's dramatically angled roofline, while adapting their own futuristic (arch-inspired) architectural embellishments. In Indiana and Michigan, the popular Yumy Burger chain erected drive-ins in which the forward lean of the buildings were exaggerated to the extreme. Reaching upward and outward, the space-age structures appeared to be poised for take-off.

Although many of the 15-cent McDonald wannabes continued to refer to themselves as drive-ins, in reality the day of the driver's seat window tray had passed. Carhops were given pink slips en masse. In the new age of fast food, even roller skates couldn't get the burger there fast enough.

Carrol's 15-cent hamburgers was a popular chain founded in Gary, Indiana, in 1956. Named after the owner's daughter, the slop-

CARROL'S FUTURISTIC BOOMERANG ROOF APPENDAGES NEVER BECAME AS FAMILIAR AS THE ICONIC ARCHES.

A CINCINNATI NEWSPAPER AD C. 1961.

ing roof was wedged between two giant turquoise boomerangs that aimed defiantly skyward. A dynamic and exciting variation on the Golden Arches theme. Their slogan promising "A serving a second," was emblazoned on the free-form sign out front. By the early Seventies, Carrol's was operating 163 restaurants nationally.

Sandy's, an Illinois-based McDonald's look-alike, first appeared in the late Fifties, and had grown to two hundred fifty units by 1972. Sandy's prided itself on "Thrift and Swift Service," and to promote their burgers used a prancing, plaid-kilted, bonnie lass (Sandy). In the Sandy's kitchens, man, meat, and machinery united in perfect harmony to produce 72 burgers in two minutes. Sandy's secret weapon: a rotating "hamburger wheel" manned by two operators upon which 48 hamburgers are assembled. The frozen patties are cooked with onion, then embellished with two squirts of ketchup, one of mustard, one dill pickle slice, and toasted buns. *Drive-in Magazine* described this as "one of the speediest methods of hamburger preparation in the country."

In 1952, an important development in burger cookery occurred in Hollywood when inventor George Read patented his revolutionary new Insta-Burger Broiler which he claimed could "deliver five hundred burgers and buns per hour." (The figure was later revised downward to four hundred fifty.) "Throw on the meat and buns and walk away!" exclaimed an ad in *American Restaurant*. "The operator places the burger in one of twelve burger baskets attached to an endless chain moving between two 'calrod' heating elements and the bun is placed underneath to absorb the burger juice when cooking. At the end of the circuit, the baskets open automatically and the burger slides into a pan of warm sauce, and the toasted bun unloads in front of the stove." This miracle of modern technology was touted as a brand-new method of food service, completely different from any other in the world.

The same year, Keith Cramer—a drive-in operator from Florida, hopped a plane to California to see firsthand what was cooking at the McDonald's stand in San Bernardino.

A few months later, Cramer, with his stepfather, purchased rights to the Insta-Burger Broiler, and opened America's first Insta-Burger King self-service drive-in in Jacksonville, Florida. In four months, they sold 55,000

A 1957 PROMOTION FOR INSTA-BURGER-KING FRANCHISES EQUIPPED WITH THE PATENTED INSTA-BURGER BROILER. THIS CONVEYOR-BELT CONTRAPTION COOKED THE BURGERS "BY RADIANT HEAT IN THE UPRIGHT POSITION."

IN 1966 "AMERICA'S FASTEST GROWING CHAIN" RAN THIS ADVERTISEMENT IN *LIFE* MAGAZINE (RIGHT).

Where 60-second service
begins with a smile...

...and ends with one

Burger King—the nation's fastest growing chain of self-service restaurants—is so delightfully different, no wonder it has caught America's fancy. Not a drive-in...not a cafeteria...not a diner—Burger King is a unique concept in restaurants, designed for America-on-the-move.

At Burger King, there are no waiters, no waiting, no tipping. Give your order and in just about 60-seconds, your hot food is ready to enjoy. The atmosphere is home-like, casual, relaxed. And you can eat inside where the weather is perfect for comfort.

The whole family will enjoy the good tasting, nourishing food—like the famous open-flame broiled *Whopper*...an exclusive Burger King creation that's a nutritionally balanced meal-in-itself—

big enough to satisfy a healthy appetite. And the kids will love those super-size shakes, too.

Wherever you go...look for the sign of the happy King-on-a-Bun. It's the sign of good food...60-second service and pleasingly low prices. That's Burger King—Home of the *Whopper*.

America's fastest-growing chain of self-service restaurants

ALABAMA Birmingham · Mobile	**GEORGIA** Atlanta · Augusta Savannah	**MICHIGAN** Ann Arbor · Flint Lansing · Detroit	**OHIO** · Cincinnati **PENNSYLVANIA** Broomall · Conshohocken	**WISCONSIN** · Milwaukee **PUERTO RICO** Greater San Juan	**International Headquarters: Miami, Florida**
COLORADO Colorado Springs · Denver	**ILLINOIS** Champaign Chicagoland (44 stores)	**MINNESOTA** Minneapolis/St. Paul	Harrisburg · King of Prussia **SOUTH CAROLINA** Anderson		
CONN. · Waterbury	**INDIANA** · Gary	**MISSOURI** · St. Louis	Charleston · Columbia Greenville · Spartanburg		
DEL. · Wilmington	**KANSAS** · Kansas City	**NEW JERSEY** · Edison	**TENNESSEE**		
FLORIDA Fort Lauderdale · Hialeah	**KENTUCKY** · Louisville	**NEW YORK** · Queens Hempstead, L. I.	Knoxville · Nashville Memphis (Jolly King)		
Greater Miami · Hollywood Jacksonville · Key West	**LOUISIANA** Baton Rouge · New Orleans Shreveport	**NORTH CAROLINA** Asheville · Charlotte	**TEXAS** Dallas · Denton · Houston		
Ocala · Pensacola Pompano · W. Palm Beach	**MASSACHUSETTS** Greater Boston	Greensboro · High Point Winston Salem	**VIRGINIA** Fairfax · Norfolk		

BURGER KING®
HOME OF THE **WHOPPER**

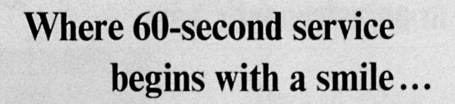

18-cent hamburgers, and began to draw up plans to franchise Insta-Burger-Kings.

In 1956, Cramer opened his tenth Insta-Burger King in Jacksonville. Now there were 47 restaurants operating in 22 states with others opening in rapid succession.

On the roof of each of the earliest restaurants was a large tower that was visible several blocks away. Atop the tower, seated on an enormous hamburger, was a jolly old king styled in neon and grasping an oversized milkshake. In 1957, the pylon tower was eliminated by Miami franchisee David Edgarton, and the colorful symbol of the seated king was used in a large sign near the street. The buildings were also redesigned to reflect the prevailing spirit of modernism. The new, more exuberant structure boasted two bright red parallel "handlebars" which appeared to burst through the roof.

In 1958, problems with Read's Insta-broiler were becoming apparent. Burger juices were dripping onto the heating elements causing them to corrode. With his partner James McLamore, Edgarton designed a new broiler and arranged for the Sani-Serv company of Indianapolis (inventors of the soft-ice-cream machine) to manufacture it for them. The new design dispensed with the troublesome heating elements by transporting the burgers horizontally over gas flames. This development

would ultimately become the chain's biggest claim to fame. The "flame broiled" burger had arrived.

The new broiler was designed to cook bigger burgers. Inspired by the brisk sales of an oversize sandwich served at the What-A-Burger stand up the street, Edgerton devised a monumental new menu addition, and named it the Whopper. This extraordinary 29-cent king-size deluxe burger concoction proved such a success that Burger King ("Insta" was dropped at this time) restaurants were soon promoting themselves as The Home of the Whopper. A change of pace for those burgermaniacs who had grown accustomed to devouring several of the modest 15-centers in one sitting, the Whopper was a plentiful patty on a 4½-inch bun, packed with trimmings galore. The original was a real treat and a mess to eat, and early Burger King ads carried the slogan "It takes two hands to handle a Whopper."

Over the next decade, the network of Burger King franchises continued its national expansion at a phenomenal rate. In 1977, the two thousandth restaurant opened in Hawaii, and by 1991 there were 6,300 worldwide, serving nearly two million Whoppers per day.

Utilizing the flame-broiler developed for Burger King, Sani-Serv president Frank Thomas in 1958 launched the remarkably successful Burger Chef chain in Indianapolis. The "proof-tested" (applying Burger King's experience and expertise) drive-ins, like their predecessors, dispensed burgers, shakes, and fries from outdoor walk-up windows. The turquoise, orange, and white Burger Chef buildings were attention-getters by virtue of a diamond-shaped orange frame which extended from the base of the building, through the roof to a point on top above the Burger Chef logo. The sign near the entrance mimicked the diamond motif, with a neon cartoony chef, and the company trademark, "We sell millions nationwide." (Who's counting?)

The Burger Chef system expanded at break-

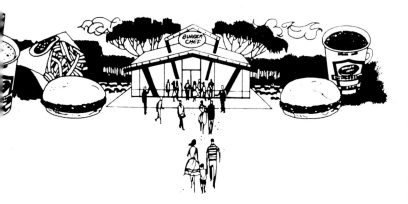

BURGER CHEF'S FANCIFUL BURGER SHRINES, DESIGNED BY HARRY E. COOLER, WERE WELCOME SIGHTS TO MIDWESTERNERS FOR OVER TWENTY YEARS.

neck speed and within five years there were two hundred fifty restaurants in twenty-eight states. In 1963, Miss America, Jackie Mayer, dropped in for lunch at her hometown Burger Chef in Sandusky, Ohio, and was presented with a gold credit card good at any Burger Chef in America. Fortunately for Jackie, by the end of the decade there would be a thousand for her to choose from.

In 1960, William Hardee opened an immensely popular quick service hamburger stand in Greenville, North Carolina, which was destined to grow into a franchising empire. Featuring 15-cent "jet service charco-broiled hamburgers" the Hardee's chain utilized a "revolutionary" charcoal broiler whose water-purifying system was said to "float away grease and keep the charcoal free from impurities."

Offering yet another newfangled technological innovation in hamburger cookery, a national chain of Biff Burgers featuring "roto-broiled" 15-cent hamburgers emerged in Florida in the early Sixties. At Biff's, the burgers were rotated under glowing quartz heating tubes which the manufacturer described as "just like a space-heater."

The Jack in the Box chain got its start in San Diego in 1951 as an early pioneer of the drive-thru concept. In the Fifties and Sixties they become known nationally for "insured quality hamburgers" as well as their distinctive "pop goes the weasel" trademark clown. This mas-

cot was wired for sound, and incorporated into the electronic ordering system.

As countless others hopped on the self-service bandwagon, hoping to duplicate the McDonald's success, new hamburger franchise systems were announced nearly every other day. Kelly's Jet System 15-cent hamburgers spread rapidly through the Southeast in the early Sixties, while Golden Point and Henry's got things cooking in the Midwest. The Tennessee chain of Jiffy Drive-ins managed to keep the price of their burgers down to 12 cents by skimping on the fries. "The french fry cartons were specially designed to give a much larger appearance than what is actually there," confessed founder J. W. Still.

The Steer-In chain made its appearance coast to coast about the same time, as did Winky's in Pennsylvania, Burger Queen in Florida, Jack's Hamburgers in Alabama, Carter's in Michigan ("Six in a bag for a buck!"), and Wetson's in New York and New Jersey. Fif-

BURGER CHEF'S AMBITIOUS PLANS FOR NATIONAL EXPANSION WERE HIGHLIGHTED IN A 1967 SALES BROCHURE.

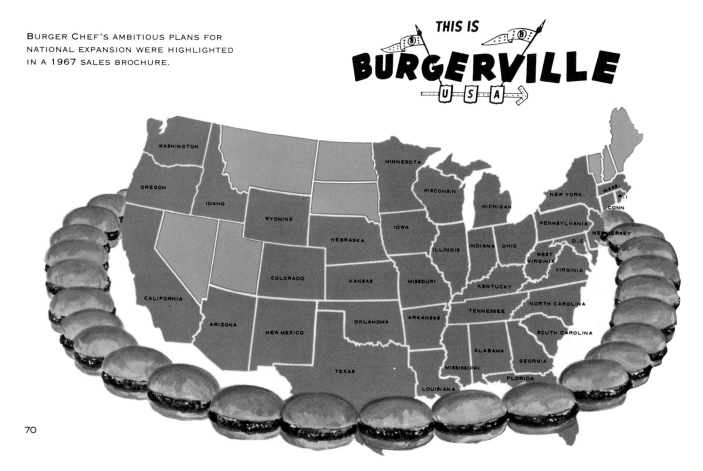

HARDEE'S 15-CENT "CHARCO-BROILED" BURGERS TOOK OFF IN NORTH CAROLINA IN 1960.

teen-cent Satellite Hamburger Systems took off in the Indianapolis area in 1962. Two years later, Washington State hamburger man George Propstra was making plans to franchise his fourth Burgerville USA in Vancouver, and the Burger Boy Food-O-Rama chain of Ohio announced an ambitious schedule for expansion. National Carfeteria Systems of Minneapolis unveiled their O.K. Big Burger franchise in 1967, complete with a custom-designed cooking unit capable of producing a burger every three seconds.

Larry Lattomus entered the 15-cent franchising sweepstakes with the opening of his first Mr. Fifteen self-service drive-ins in Muncie, Indiana, in 1960. But the days of 15-cent hamburgers were nearly at an end. In 1967,

BURGERS AT BIG CITY PRICES ON CHICAGO'S WEST SIDE, 1967.

IN 1964 THE NAME SAID IT ALL AT THE STEER INN IN PLAINFIELD, NEW JERSEY.

escalating labor and food costs prompted the startling announcement from the McDonald's Corporation that they would be raising the price of their hamburgers to 18 cents. Referred to as Black Wednesday by the national press, it was earth-shattering news to hamburger purveyors and consumers alike.

Almost immediately, all others followed suit, and for a time the mean price of a burger held steady at about 19 cents. To the owners of Whoopee Burger in Chicago, it was no big deal, they had been charging 19 cents all along. Burger Chef managed to absorb the increased costs for several months during which time they launched a national ad campaign promoting themselves as "America's number one 15-cent hamburger chain." The

DAG'S BEEFY BOY BURGER—
AN INSTITUTION IN WASHINGTON
STATE SINCE THE MID-FIFTIES.

title was short-lived, however. By the year's end they too would find it necessary to remove or disguise the 15-cent price tag featured prominently on roadside signs nationwide.

As the Sixties wound down, the hamburger chains faced rising beef costs and an intensely competitive climate. Along the way, many made concessions to help ease the profit squeeze. Increasingly, preportioned frozen hamburgers and fries were served, and the "fresh ground" variety became an endangered species. Most burger chains did not survive; those that did spent heavily on advertising, and were willing to adapt to changes in public tastes and lifestyles. By 1970, a shakeout in the hamburger business was already under way.

A BURGER KING CLONE WITH AN
OFFER FEW COULD REFUSE.

BURGER BATTLES

THINGS GET HOT IN HEAVEN

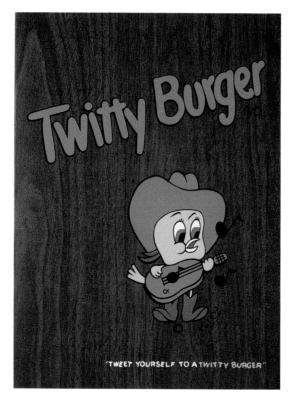

IN 1970, COUNTRY MUSIC LEGEND CONWAY TWITTY BRIEFLY ENTERED THE BURGER BATTLE ZONE, SELLING TWITTY BURGERS IN OKLAHOMA.

Whatever became of Baron Von Burger and his high-flying Biplane Burgers? Sad to say, he went down with his chain, as did the Lone Ranger and his Ranchburgers, Conway and his Twitty Burgers, and Li'l Abner's supersize Yokumburgers. They, along with innumerable others, were counted among the casualties of the Great Hamburger Wars.

Late in the Sixties, after twenty years of relative stability, beef prices began to rise, making it increasingly difficult to produce cheap burgers. In 1971 the price of a burger served under the arches jumped to 20 cents.

Although the expansion of the larger chains continued unabated, it was often at the expense of the smaller regional operators. McDonald's and Burger King meticulously researched population and marketing trends before deciding on new locations for their restaurants, often placing them across the street from the established local hamburger stands. And only the strong survived.

Both Burger King and McDonald's redesigned their restaurants in response to dramatic changes in the public mood. America's

SUPERSTAR WARS BY JIM KINGSTON (RIGHT).

McDonald's "CANDY-STRIPED" RESTAURANTS AND BURGER KING'S JOLLY OLD MASCOT WERE NOT ALLOWED TO STICK AROUND FOR THE SEVENTIES.

"YUMY" BURGER WAS A MIDWEST CASUALTY BY 1972.

WHEN THE HEAVY HITTERS OF HAMBURGERLAND BEGAN SPENDING MILLIONS ON TELEVISION ADVERTISING, MANY OF THE SMALLER OPERATIONS WERE RENDERED DEFENSELESS.

fascination with the future, and the daring, offbeat architecture it had inspired, was waning. The glowing, blinking, pulsing, flashing, roadside strip had become a neon hodgepodge, and communities began to pass ordinances to put an end to it.

The new generation of fast-burger emporiums was designed with the public's environmental concerns in mind. A kinder, gentler, less conspicuous style emerged. The toned down structures lacked whimsy, but fit unobtrusively into Anytown U.S.A. . . . like the church, the bank, or the schoolhouse. Neon kings were banished forever, replaced by simpler, less energetic burger logos and signage. The age of fun and fantasy in hamburger land had come to pass.

McDonald's and the other chains decided to make a concerted effort to capture the family

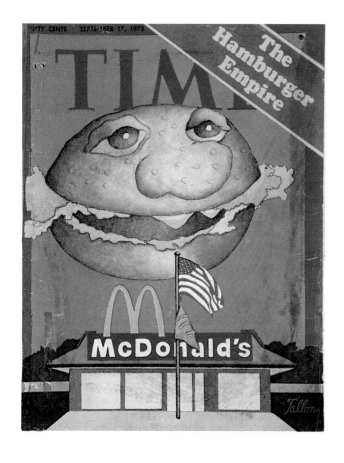

market. "That meant going for the kids," explained McDonald's in 1973. "We decided to use television, so we created Ronald McDonald." Ronald made his first public appearance in Washington, D.C., in 1963, and was played by television weather personality (and former Bozo sidekick Clarabelle the Clown) Willard Scott. Two years later, the McDonald's "You deserve a break today" theme song placed second only to the national anthem in terms of public awareness.

In 1972, Hardee's increased their arsenal with the acquisition of Sandy's 225-unit hamburger chain, while McDonald's signs were all aglow with their own good news: "More than ten billion burgers served." They reported a net profit of one billion dollars, and had surpassed the U.S. Army to become the nation's largest dispenser of meals. A year later, they were opening a new restaurant every day, and had an advertising budget of $50 million.

In 1967, the 274-store Burger King empire was bought by Pillsbury Company, for $18 million. A new ad jingle—"The bigger the burger, the better the burger"—struck a chord with hungry consumers, and Whopper sales kept hopping. The same year (no doubt in response to the gaining popularity of the heftier hamburgers), McDonald's unveiled a new weapon, the Big Mac—a double-decker Big Boy clone consisting of two all-beef patties with cheese, pickles, onions, and special sauce on a sesame seed bun.

In 1971, Jack in the Box pulled a fast-food fast one when it introduced its Jumbo Jack hamburger with the help of six-year-old television spokesperson Rodney Allen Rippy, who experienced great difficulty getting his mouth

WHEN RODNEY ALLEN RIPPY HAWKED THE HARD-TO-HANDLE JUMBO JACK FOR JACK IN THE BOX IN 1971, SALES SURGED.

around the bodacious burger. Within months, Hardee's Big Burger Deluxe took aim at the brawny burger niche and hit their mark. Twenty years later Hardee's honchos proudly boast that "the B.B.D. remains our flagship burger." In a bewildering burger development, in the spring of 1973, Burger King's Big Plain hit the stands. This naked quarter-pound patty was a plain hamburger on a bun with *nothing* on it, and, stranger still, it cost more than the heavily garnished Whopper. The Big Plain was a big bomb. That same year, McDonald's added the Quarter Pounder to their burger battery.

In 1976, with 120 restaurants operating in the East, Carrol's recognized that they

RONALD MCDONALD THEN AND NOW. WILLARD SCOTT STARTED IT ALL IN 1963 (TOP). THE 1992 EDITION CARRIES ON THE TRADITION.

IN 1968, THIRTY-ONE YEARS AFTER BOB WIAN COOKED UP HIS FIRST DOUBLE-DECKER BIG BOY, MCDONALD'S ANNOUNCED THEIR ENTRY INTO THE FIELD.

McDonald's introduces Big Mac.
A meal disguised as a sandwich.

It's as good as it is big. Under scoops of our own special sauce are two patties of lean 100% beef. (Guaranteed by Parents' Magazine . . . or your money back.)

There's a slice of melty cheddar-blend cheese; some fresh crisp lettuce; and crunchy dill pickle slices. All wrapped up in a freshly toasted sesame seed bun.

Come now, bring us your bigger than average appetite.

It's all at your kind of place.

McDonald's

could no longer compete with the national chains, and surrendered unconditionally. "We couldn't lick them, so we joined them," admitted chairman Herbert Slotnick, after announcing plans to convert the Carrol's chain to Burger King franchises.

White Tower made earnest attempts to adapt to changing tastes by relocating to suburban areas with larger self-serve restaurants. But by the mid-Seventies these original hamburger pioneers grew war-weary and began to franchise Burger Kings in the East. Today the once regal Towers number less than five.

In 1967, General Foods gobbled up America's third-largest organization of hamburger eateries, the 600-restaurant Burger Chef group, for $15 million. The following year, all 280 links in the Jack-in-the-Box chain were acquired by the Ralston Purina Company. Amid this mounting frenzy of consolidation and acquisition, when most industry observers were convinced that America could not absorb another burger stand, an unlikely David appeared to do battle with the mighty Goliaths of Burgerland.

David Thomas's goal at twelve was to own and operate a "really good hamburger stand."

THE FIRST WENDY'S OLD FASHIONED HAMBURGERS OPENED IN COLUMBUS, OHIO, IN 1969 (ABOVE).

WHITE TOWER'S ILL-FATED EFFORTS TO KEEP PACE WITH CHANGING TASTES INCLUDED THIS 1972 UNIT IN RALEIGH, NORTH CAROLINA (TOP).

YES, HAMBURGER LOVERS, THERE REALLY IS A WENDY! THE FOUNDER'S DAUGHTER. SHOWN HERE IN 1970.

DAVE THOMAS'S PERSONAL HANKERING FOR A FRESH "HOT 'N JUICY" HAMBURGER PROMPTED THE REMARKABLE RISE OF THE WENDY'S CHAIN IN THE 1970S.

After working with Colonel Harlan Sanders, and operating three Kentucky Fried Chicken restaurants in Columbus, Ohio, he sold the franchises back to the Colonel in 1962, and became a thirty-five-year-old millionaire. He then went stalking his childhood fantasy.

Well aware that made-to-order hamburgers were becoming increasingly difficult to find in the age of the frozen, pattied, prewrapped, factory-built burgers, Dave wanted to return to the "old fashioned" staple. With the mantra "quality is our recipe," he entered the burger battleground in 1969, and named the restaurant after his daughter Wendy.

Wendy's old-fashioned hamburgers were hot, juicy, fresh, square, and personally customized with any of 256 combinations of condiments. Lettuce, tomato, onions, pickle, mayonnaise, ketchup, and mustard were yours for the asking at no extra cost. Dave's hamburger intuition paid off. During the Seventies, Wendy's went from relative midwestern obscurity to become a tough contender. By 1976, Dave had assembled a national fighting force of 925 hamburger stands, whose pseudo-Tiffany lamps and Gay Nineties decor reinforced the spirit of the good old days. By 1979 a new Wendy's burgery was opening every sixteen hours.

Wendy's burgers go directly from the cook to the customer. The grill chef is trained to keep a watchful eye on the door, and an appropriate number of patties cooking. At Wendy's, they wouldn't be caught dead warming their buns under heat lamps.

After the remarkable rise of Wendy's, along came sound-alikes Cindy's and Judy's. All were hoping against all odds that one more

IN '64—BEFORE THE GREAT WAR—SWIFT'S PREMIUM SOUGHT TO UNITE THE WORLD WITH AMERICA'S "SYMBOL OF FRIENDSHIP."

BURGER CHEF'S DUO, INTRODUCED IN THE SEVENTIES, WERE AIMED AT RONALD'S GROWING LEGIONS.

window of opportunity might remain open in the oversaturated hamburger market, but they were soon listed among the casualties in the increasingly bitter battle of the burgers.

In 1979, the lines were drawn, and the big three, McDonald's, Burger King, and Wendy's, squared off to fight it out over the airwaves. McDonald's, experiencing declining profit margins, still commanded a 20 percent share of the market (more than twice that of number two ranked Burger King). Industry wide, analysts predicted a major shakeout, due in part to a 30 percent jump in beef prices, and an increase in the minimum wage. Of even greater concern to McDonald's were the humbling conclusions drawn from their own study indicating that consumers rated Burger King and Wendy's hamburgers higher on quality as "hot and tasty food."

On the defensive, McDonald's mounted a $200 million advertising McBlitz. Meanwhile, Burger King moved forward with its $50 million campaign, touting the Whopper as "the best darn burger in the whole wide world,"

THE MAGICAL BURGER KING MATERIALIZED IN THE EARLY EIGHTIES, ALONG WITH A FRONTAL ASSAULT ON MCDONALD'S COOKING METHODS.

A 1982 RESTAURANT TRAY LINER WITH A FASCINATING STORY TO TELL.

and introduced a new weapon: The Magical Burger King who—it was hoped—would effectively counter McDonald's kid-pleasing clown, Ronald. As family traffic was rerouted through the magical kingdom, McDonald's began serving breakfast.

By 1981 the big three were collectively cooking up 60 percent of all fast-food hamburgers sold. The following year, Burger King launched "the Great Hamburger War of 1982," with a sweeping all-out ad attack that posed the $80 million question: "Aren't you hungry?" The hard-hitting television campaign included an explosive comparative advertising blitz code-named B.O.B. (Battle of the Bur-

gers). The aggressive maneuver assailed Wendy's and McDonald's for their burger-cooking methods (frying), claiming that in coast-to-coast taste tests, Burger King beat their competitors by two to one for "best taste overall."

Burger King spent $18 million on the battle of the burgers alone. Word of the impending attack began to circulate two weeks before the commercials were set to air. McDonald's and Wendy's were not amused. McDonald's sought (unsuccessfully) a federal restraining order halting the television spots. Within days Wendy's called for a "national hamburger taste test" (both parties declined) while filing a lawsuit against Burger King, and seeking

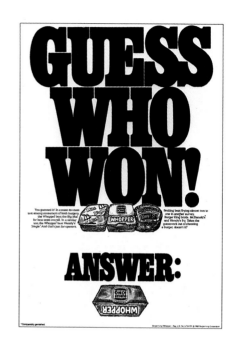

SUBWAY BILLBOARDS AND MAGAZINE ADS ANNOUNCED THE VICTORY.

$25 million in damages.

The McDonald's suit disputed Burger King's contention that their burgers were, in fact, "broiled," stating that after the burgers are flame-cooked, they are "often steamed and re-heated or warmed in microwave ovens before sales to consumers." The burger wars made the network news, and it wasn't long before everybody was taking sides in the battle.

One month after the war began, in an out-of-court settlement, all parties signed an un-easy truce (sums undisclosed) in which Burger King agreed to a temporary cease-fire. At the end of the mortal media conflict, Burger King estimated that project B.O.B. generated $20 to $30 million in free publicity, and by the time the big three squared off again in 1984, Burger King had realized a sales spurt of 30 percent.

This time Wendy's took the offensive. Their top secret weapon, a five-foot-tall octogenar-ian and former manicurist from Illinois, Clara Peller, proved a great leader, and war hero.

The attack began January 9, 1984, with a thirty-second television commercial featuring three elderly women eyeing a giant hamburger bun. When the overly ample bun is removed, a petite, pathetic patty is revealed, prompting an irritated Ms. Peller to demand: "Where's the beef?" Those three immortal words cata-pulted into the American vernacular.

The slogan found new life and a deeper meaning when presidential candidate Walter Mondale attacked the "new ideas" theme of his rival, Gary Hart, as all talk and no sub-stance. In a nationally televised debate he de-manded of Hart: "Where's the beef?"

In three more deliciously funny commercials Clara continued to lead the Wendy's forces triumphantly through the burger battles for several more months, as sales of Wendy's big beefy burgers shot up 36 percent. Meanwhile, Burger King announced a revamped Whopper with more meat and a smaller bun. This was *not* (they claimed) a response to Wendy's but

because their own extensive taste tests had concluded (coincidentally) that "customers had long indicated that there was too much bun and that perhaps they'd like more meat." Burger King spent $30 million introducing the new beefier Whopper (increased from 3.6 ounces to 4.2 ounces) that they unveiled with major hamburger hoopla in July 1985. However, a mere year later, they quietly reduced the size of the patty from 4.2 to 4 ounces, and expanded the bun again, without a word. Hardee's, the nation's number four burger chain, entered the crossfire by calling attention to the secretly scaled-down Whopper, in television ads showing a king magically shrinking a big burger to a tiny size. Burger King explained the reversal as a move they found necessary to "hold the burger together better."

Wendys's most powerful piece of artillery, a sassy sense of humor, continued to inspire successful campaigns and to win over legions of fresh burger devotees. In 1986, they clobbered the competition again with an ad parodying a Russian fashion show, and a series of ads in which an interviewer asks individuals to choose between a fresh Wendy's hamburger and one packed in plastic. A woman chooses Hamburger B explaining: "Virtually everything I own is covered in plastic."

This latest round of wacky attacks from Wendy's all but eclipsed the introduction of McDonald's much heralded innovation, their first ever hamburger with lettuce and tomato, the McD.L.T. This earth-shattering menu addition was considered such a McDonald's milestone that a patented, two-part styrofoam container was developed to keep the lettuce and tomato separate and cool on one side, while the beef remained miraculously warm and wonderful on the other. In a uniquely hands-on hamburger experience, the consumer would then merge the two halves. For some still unfathomable and perplexing reason, the cheese was placed in the cold side

where it remained as cool and crispy as the greenery. The McD.L.T. never really caught on, and was given an early retirement in 1991.

While Wendy's was gaining ground and McDonald's was rolling out the McD.L.T. amid great fanfare, Burger King unleashed the highly visible and extremely unpopular Herb (the nerd) campaign at a price of $40 million. Herb, the bookish bespectacled dork, was apparently so terminally unhip that he had never tasted a Whopper. If Burger King had hoped to duplicate Wendy's success by creating offbeat, humorous commercials, and an unlikely hero, they had failed miserably.

In 1987, in a stunning departure from its predictably wholesome marketing approach, McDonald's introduced an unconventional hamburger hawker named Mac Tonight. Unlike hapless Herb, moon-faced Mac was a terminally hip lounge singer extraordinaire who captured the imagination of the nation.

After floundering with Herb and a barrage of similarly ineffective campaigns, Burger

HAPLESS HERB THE NERD
FIRED BLANKS FOR BURGER KING
IN A 1986 ADVERTISING BLITZ.

TAKING AN ACADEMIC APPROACH TO THE BUSINESS OF BURGERS, MCDONALD'S FOUNDED HAMBURGER UNIVERSITY IN 1961 IN ELK GROVE, ILLINOIS, WHERE MANAGERS EARN A BACHELOR OF HAMBURGEROLOGY DEGREE.

King, in retreat, resumed the winning strategies that focused on its strengths: flame broiling and the advantages of "having it your way." In the late Eighties, it surrendered the kiddie market to McDonald's, putting the Magical Burger King character to rest. In 1988 Britain's Grand Metropolitan purchased Burger King Corporation, and the following year acquired Wimpy's restaurants in Europe. Meanwhile, McDonald's marched on, spending millions on playgrounds and flashy ads directed primarily at children. Conversely, in 1990, while continuing to target the adult market, Wendy's discovered an unlikely new spokesperson in its founder, good old boy Dave Thomas, who was not nearly as much fun as Clara, but almost as effective. When homespun Dave appeared in commercials hyping deluxe combinations of his hot and juicy hamburgers, sales skyrocketed by nearly a third.

In 1982, Hardee's purchased the 650-store Burger Chef operation in the Midwest, and converted most of them to Hardee's outlets. In 1990 they absorbed the Roy Rogers chain, significantly increasing their firepower in the East, and vaulting them ahead of Wendy's as the third-place giant of the burger business. That year, the Hardee's system of 4,022 restaurants celebrated the thirtieth birthday of their Jet System Charco-burgers.

Into the Nineties, the ferocious battle for burger-bucks wages on, as periods of relative calm are followed by nasty price wars, and cutthroat competition. Broiling, frying, and freshness remain the major confrontational issues, while attention-getting, newfangled burger concoctions have become the weapons of choice, and menus are expanded to attract new customers. As the burger superpowers continue aggressively to pursue an agenda of international expansion, the great American hamburger wars will undoubtedly, eventually, erupt into global conflict. It's only a matter of time.

McDONALD'S DISCOVERED TOMATOES (FINALLY) IN 1986, WITH THE INTRODUCTION OF THE McD.L.T. A SPECIAL DUAL PACKAGE WAS DEEMED NECESSARY.

A CHARISMATIC SMOOTHIE IN DARK GLASSES, MAC TONIGHT MADE THE SCENE IN 1987.

ARCHITECTURE
AND SIGNAGE

BURGERIZE
HERE
GREEN HORN

THE BURGER THAT ATE L.A. IS A MELROSE AVENUE LANDMARK DESIGNED BY SOLBERG AND LOWE IN 1989.

EARLY IN THE TWENTIETH CENTURY HAMBURGER HABITATS WERE REFRESHING ROADSIDE VISIONS.

The exalted hamburger is at the heart of a diverse and dazzling array of architectural treasures and oddities. The "burger palaces," "joints," and "stands" and the dynamic signage that they employed, represent a remarkable facet of our culturally rich hamburger heritage. From neon temples to roadside diners, all are to be cherished for providing absorbing visual stimulation and a festive environment in which to "get Burgerized."

WHIZBURGER NEON. PORTLAND, OREGON, 1980.

An A&W Root Beer stand around 1950. Founded in 1922, A&W was one of the first food franchises.

Short Stop Hamburgers, Belleville, New Jersey, 1975.

The Ranch House Drive-in, Louisville, Kentucky.

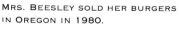

Mrs. Beesley sold her burgers in Oregon in 1980.

Don's Place still thrives in Burbank, California, and buttered burgers are offered in North Attleboro, Massachusetts.

Johnie's Fat Boy stands in Downey, California, in 1993. Formerly Harvey's Broiler—a spectacular drive-in oasis.

BURGERVILLE, U.S.A., VANCOUVER, WASHINGTON, 1980.

ANOTHER FAT BURGER BOY FROM INDIANA, 1974.

PETER PAN (ORIGINALLY THE POPULAR CHAR-BERT'S DRIVE-IN), COLUMBUS, OHIO, 1988.

THIS EIGHTY-FOOT GIANT SOLD HICKORY BURGERS IN MALIBU, CALIFORNIA, UNTIL A MAKE-OVER IN THE LATE EIGHTIES TRANSFORMED HIM INTO A TRENDY TACO TENDER.

MAMA POSSUM'S BURGERS, THE LEGEND AND LANDMARK. DANVILLE, VIRGINIA.

SUPERMAN'S FATHER KNEW A THING OR TWO ABOUT FAST SERVICE. HIS ROCKET BURGERS WERE 15 CENTS. LOCATION UNKNOWN.

CHARLIE BROWN'S BURGER HOUSE BEAUTIFIED THE LANDSCAPE IN CARROLTON, TEXAS,
FOR THIRTEEN YEARS PRIOR TO DEMOLITION IN 1983. ANOTHER ICON OF GOOD TASTE,
JOHN'S RESTAURANT (INSET) ON ROUTE 130 IN NEW JERSEY, C. 1973.

BIG CHIEF'S WAHOOOO HAMBURGS,
DOWAGIAC, MICHIGAN, C. 1990.

PUTTING THE FINISHING TOUCHES ON A LARGER-THAN-LIFE BURGER WHICH INTRODUCED
MCDONALD'S QUARTER POUNDER ON BILLBOARDS IN 1972.

BURGER VISIONS

Over the years, the bold and colorful aesthetic of the hamburger has inspired a rich array of arresting imagery and creative interpretations. The famous profile is well represented in a variety of media, from matchbook and album cover art to newspaper accounts and roadside billboards. Often the burger's universal appeal was exploited in advertising campaigns for companion products. Peachy cheeseburgers were promoted by America's peach growers, while soft drink, beer, and condiment manufacturers have long recognized the inherent marketing potential of the satisfying sandwich. This appetizing array of commercial art and graphics, as well as the revelatory burger visions of contemporary artists, reflects the unlimited possibilities of the glorious hamburger.

A COLORFUL GRAPHIC PROMOTED BURGERS AT REDUCED RATES IN THE LATE SIXTIES.

BEVERAGE COMPANIES KNEW HOW TO ADD APPEAL TO THEIR PRODUCTS.

SQUIRT
Quenches
Quicker

1948

OCTOBER						
SUN	MON	TUE	WED	THU	FRI	SAT
					1	2
3	4	5	6	7	8	9
10	11	12	13	14	15	16
17	18	19	20	21	22	23
24 31	25	26	27	28	29	30

NOVEMBER						
SUN	MON	TUE	WED	THU	FRI	SAT
	1	2	3	4	5	6
7	8	9	10	11	12	13
14	15	16	17	18	19	20
21	22	23	24	25	26	27
28	29	30				

DECEMBER						
SUN	MON	TUE	WED	THU	FRI	SAT
			1	2	3	4
5	6	7	8	9	10	11
12	13	14	15	16	17	18
19	20	21	22	23	24	25
26	27	28	29	30	31	

COMPLIMENTS OF THE

BAND BOX

HAMBURGER SHOPS

CLOSE COVER BEFORE STRIKING

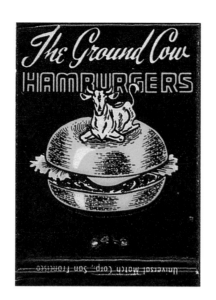

The Ground Cow
HAMBURGERS

Universal Match Corp. San Francisco

FRIEDL'S
California
HAMBURGER

THE OHIO MATCH CO., WADSWORTH, OHIO
MADE IN U.S.A.

Denver's Best
HAMBURGERS

GEORGE
WEBB
®

HAMBURGER
PARLORS

Gracie O's
IRISH HAMBURGER
THE FLAVOR SECRET IS IN THE
SHAMROCK DRESSING

CHARCOAL BROILED
for your health's sake

Frontier
DRIVE-INS

CLOSE COVER BEFORE STRIKING MATCH

Open Day & Night

Famous SUBWAY
HAMBURGERS

MOTORCYCLE DELIVERY
Phone 2-1928
981 LOUISIANA AVENUE
SHREVEPORT, LA.

ROYAL
STEAKBURGER

CLOSE COVER BEFORE STRIKING

CURB
SERVICE

THE PRINTED MATCHBOOK COVER REPRESENTS ONE OF THE RICHEST RESOURCES FOR HAMBURGER GRAPHICS AND ILLUSTRATION. THESE APPEALING VISUALS DEMANDED ATTENTION WITH THE PROMISE OF A HEAVENLY HAMBURGER EXPERIENCE.

THIS 1956 BILLBOARD ENCOURAGED CHICAGOANS TO "GO OUT" FOR THEIR CHEESEBURGERS, AND WAS COSPONSORED BY THE CHICAGO RESTAURANT ASSOCIATION. GIVEN THE CLOSE CAMARADERIE BETWEEN THE AUTO AND THE BURGER, ROADSIDE BILLBOARDS PRESENTED AN OBVIOUS MEANS OF EFFECTIVELY HYPING THE HAMBURGER.

A 1978 SUBWAY POSTER ECHOED THE STATION'S TILE MOTIF.

THE QUICKWAY DINER OFF ROUTE 17 IN NEW YORK ENTICED NORTHBOUND MOTORISTS WITH THIS WHOLESOME ALL-AMERICAN IMAGE FROM THE 1950S.

THE BUILDING AS BURGER BILLBOARD. AMSTERDAM AVENUE, NEW YORK, 1979.

A CANADIAN BILLBOARD CAPITALIZED ON THE POPULARITY OF TWO AMERICAN HEROES.

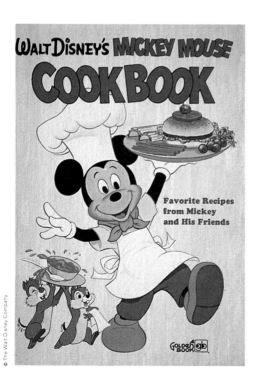

MICKEY MOUSE'S SPECIAL HAMBURGER RECIPE WAS REVEALED IN THIS 1975 PUBLICATION.

IN 1942, BUGS BUNNY AND PORKY PIG COULD BE FOUND, HAMBURGERS IN HAND, AT THE CORNER LUNCH COUNTER.

THE WORLD'S FIRST BURGERMANIAC, WIMPY HAD ONLY ONE THING ON HIS CRAFTY CONSCIENCE.

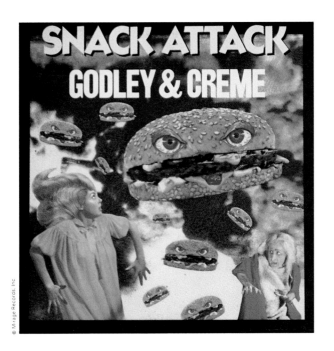

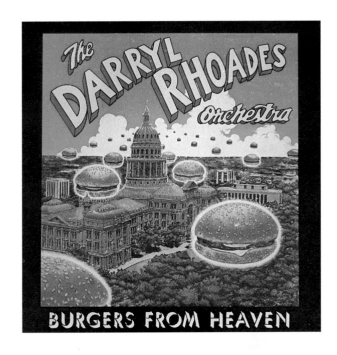

VINTAGE FILLMORE WEST POSTER FROM THE SIXTIES
FEATURING CHUCK BERRY AND HAMBURGER PSYCHEDELIA.

ALBUM COVER GRAPHICS WERE AN IDEAL OUTLET
FOR FANTASTIC BURGER VISIONS.

Music adds magic
. . . to the hamburger heaven

HAMBURGER HEADLINES

LIKE MOST SUPERSTARS HOUNDED BY THE MEDIA, THE HAMBURGER IS NO STRANGER TO CONTROVERSY. IT IS OFTEN ALLEGED TO BE THE CENTER OF BIZARRE SCENERIOS AND FREQUENTLY SEEN IN THE COMPANY OF AMERICA'S MOST CELEBRATED CITIZENS.

CHEESEBURGER KILLS SPACE ALIEN!

Fatal fast-food feeding frenzy

© Weekly World News

INSIDE MICHAEL JACKSON'S BEDROOM
EXCLUSIVE PHOTOS IN COLOR

GLOBE Lose 5 lbs a week on the amazing **BURGER DIET**

How to make your man cr...
— FOR HIS OWN GOOD

© Globe

Fidel's fast food joints popping up all over Cuba

Castro selling burgers made from earthworm

WHERE'S THE BEEF?

By LAUREL BOWIE
Staff writer

Dinghat dictator Fidel Castro has opened 50 state-run hamburger joints in Havana, but the burgers featherbrained Fidel's frying up are only 20 percent beef — and 80 percent ground earthworms!

Insiders say the kooky Cuban kingpin wouldn't be caught dead wolfing down a wormburger himself. Instead, the Big Mac gobbling bag of wind has all his burgers flown in from Big Macs and quarter Pound. a Miami McDonald's...

This woman saw Presley at Kalamazoo Burger King

BURGER KING

Dinner Dancing With Hamburger Social "Must"

Beefy Boys Play In Lavish Bun Room

In a cultural coup that could leave Seattle staggering—from Twist fatigue—DAG brings together The ...mburger at his hunger ...at din- been places ...ub cel- "Let's ...en air y Boy

DAG's

They're hoppi... over 'bunny b...

Post Wire Services
ORLANDO, Fla. — The American Rabbit Breeders Assn. believes rabbit meat is the food of the future, but an animal rights group has vowed to fight "bunny burgers."

About 75 protesters wearing rabbit cost...

boycott," Sequoya o... yesterday. Rabbit ... missed the p...

"Rabbit is ... one of the mo... meats of the ... Ed Pelser the...

Customer on the attack — with a cheeseburger

A fast-food customer who found hair in a bacon cheeseburger hauled off and hit manager Kay McCorbin in the head with it!

"He had no reason to hit me with that burger," fumed the ...ld woman from Char... ...in the

Cannibal cow loves to eat hamburger

MIS...
Hardees restaura..., food fight began after the unidentified man complained about the hair.

On the assumption that the customer is always right she gave him another burger — which he bounced off her head.

Lightning struck him, so he ate two burgers

WOLVERINE LAKE, Mich. (AP) — David Renwick must make one heck of a hamburger.

Struck by lightning Saturday night while cooking outside, Renwick didn't take himself to the hospital until after eating a couple of the hamburgers he was grilling.

"I actually sat down and ate," Renwick, 39, said Sunday from Huron Valley Hospital in Milford, where he was being kept for observation. "It was really weird; I couldn't feel myself chewing."

Renwick said the numbness didn't begin subsiding until about midnight Saturday.

"I can remember an intense light and I remember feeling a real bad shock," he said. "I feel great now."

Cancer inhibitor identi...

Vegetarians like to remind the ... meat-eating may b... ...gerous to shown traces ... s and care... the hu... ...ay yet ma ...t. Micha... in Mad... ...nstitute ...d ham... part ...ed ef...

DOUBLE SUPER ZINGO – 1,000 WEEKLY WINNERS – Page 7

DAILY NEWS

LINK BELLYACHE TO HAMBURGERS

Story on page ?

ELVIS WAS SPOTTED CHOWING DOWN IN
KALAMAZOO AND THE QUEEN OF SOUL,
ARETHA FRANKLIN, HAS ALWAYS KNOWN
WHERE TO FIND SWEET INSPIRATION.

Ostrich burgers may be next

ciated Press

CUYAMA — Say "ostrich
and many diners might stick
ds in the sand. But a Central
a couple say the bird's
ing meat is destined to be-
gular restaurant item.
Wendy and Gary Teix-
strich meat provides
ol, low-fat, reason-
native to red meat.
eady to provide it.
xeira Ostrich Ranch
ing pairs of African
names such as Lav-
d Two Lips. The
birds mate earlier,

gers

omrades that
research has
ed meat. But
especially if
searcher at
ector of the
and identi-

ber *Car-*
ating skin

RISKO

THE BURGERMAN RESTAURANT ON CHAMBERS STREET IN MANHATTAN IN 1980. PAINTING BY THE AUTHOR.

ARCHIE AND JUGHEAD DISCUSS THE FINE ART OF THE BURGER IN 1970. THE WORK DISPLAYED IS BY DANDY WARHOG.

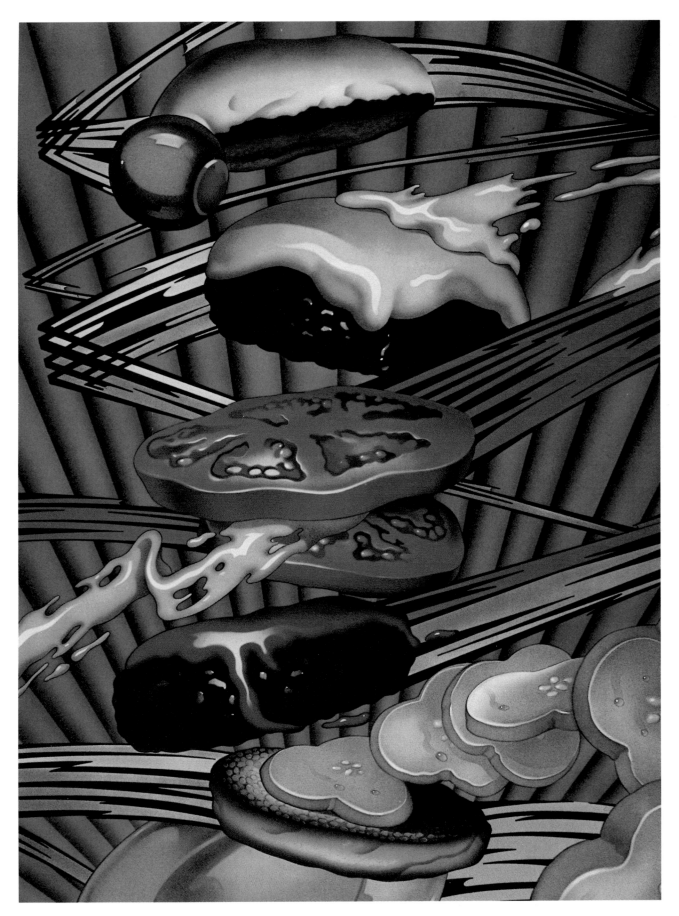

FLYING HAMBURGER, BY TODD SCHORR, 1976.

CLAES OLDENBURG'S *GIANT HAMBURGER*, 1962. PAINTED SAILCLOTH STUFFED WITH FOAM.

EGG WITH HAMBURGER YOLK, BEVERLY
CHESTERBY, 1980. PAINTED CERAMIC.

CHEESEBURGER, JERRY WILKERSON, 1980.

RADIOACTIVE REDS BY PATRICK NAGATANI/ANDREE TRACEY, 1986. POLAROID POLACOLOR PRINT.

MEMORABILIA
FUN WITH BURGERS

IN 1968, AVON OFFERED TWO SHADES OF LIP GLOSS UNDER ONE BUN.

We spend close to a third of our waking hours nourishing ourselves and that time should be savored and celebrated. What better symbol of these memorable moments is there than the most highly regarded sandwich on the planet—the tantalizingly tasteful burger.

It is a testimony to the hamburger that we have seen fit to acknowledge its estimable position by producing its likeness and form in an infinite variety of objects and artifacts. This tribute to good taste—the visual manifestation of hamburger appreciation—illuminates the burger as an important sociocultural icon and institution. One only need look around to discover that burgers abound everywhere. And for good reason.

ROTATING WIMPY MUSIC BOX PLAYS "POPEYE THE SAILOR MAN." C. 1979.

WHEN YOU CRAVE AM RADIO WITH YOUR BURGER (AND WHO DOESN'T), IT MIGHT AS WELL BE TO THE TUNE OF THE STATE-OF-THE-ART STELLARSONIC RADIOBURGER. C. 1977.

CERAMIC HAMBURGER-SHAPED COOKIE JAR. C. 1980.

THIS HAMBURGER LAMP SHEDS
LIGHT ON A VERY IMPORTANT
SUBJECT. C. 1980.

CHROME AND BRASS PAPERWEIGHT
FROM BLOOMINGDALE'S. C. 1978.

TEATIME IN HAMBURGER HEAVEN. C. 1988.

A CHEESEBURGER TELEPHONE
IS A COMFORT TO HOLD. C. 1988.

HANGING HAMBURGER
MOBILE. C. 1985.

HAMBURGER CANDLE. C. 1978.

BURGER COASTER SET. C. 1979.

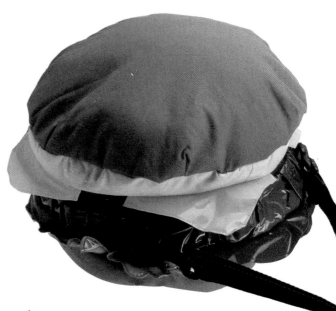

A STYLISH AND PRACTICAL HAMBURGER
SHOULDER BAG. C. 1989.

DELUXE SOAP BURGER
WITH LETTUCE-AND-
CHEESE WASHCLOTHS.
C. 1980.

BURGER HEADPHONE SET. C. 1986.

CERAMIC BURGER
BANK. C. 1983.

THIS RARE BATTERY-OPERATED
BURGER CHEF PUP SEASONS,
SHAKES, AND FLIPS HIS PATTIES.
C. 1950.

HAMBURGER PLANTER. C. 1975.

HAMBURGER TIN. C. 1985.

SALT AND PEPPER SET. C. 1992.

CHILD'S DRESS WITH
BURGERS AND FRIES. C. 1987.

MEN'S FLASHY
UNDERGARMENT. C. 1990.

GAG BIKINI BRIEFS
FOR HIM. C. 1984.

CERAMIC FIGURINE.
C. 1988.

MISCELLANEOUS HAMBURGER JEWELRY.

WRISTWATCHES C. 1987

HAMBURGER HAT BY
MANHATTAN ARTIST
HOVIK DILAKIAN. 1987.

HAMBURGER BUBBLE
GUM FROM THE
MID-EIGHTIES.

CHEESEBURGER PADDY
NOTEPAD, AND BIG MAC
PEN. C. 1986.

NOT JUST ANOTHER PRETTY BURGER.
THE PATENTED BUN-BURGER PATTY
MOLDING GIZMO. C. 1955.

A HANDY BURGER BEVERAGE
COOLER. C. 1990.

HAMBURGER CAKE
TIN. C. 1988.

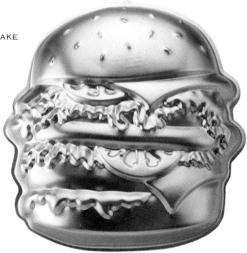

THIS HAMBURGER HOT PAD
PROVIDES HELPFUL
INSTRUCTIONS. C. 1984.

FUN WITH BURGERS

THIS WACKY WINDUP IS A HOPPING HAMBURGER. C. 1989.

THE FARTER KING "WHOOPIE CUSHION" AND THE PHONY BURGER, ARE BURGERS WITH NO TASTE.

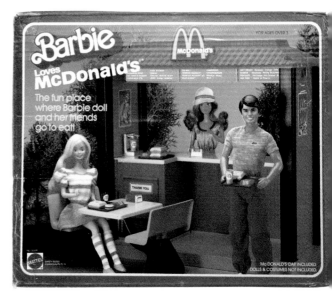

BARBIE LOVES MCDONALD'S. MINIATURE RESTAURANT INCLUDE BURGERS AND GRILL. HOURS OF FUN. C. 1984.

SUPER MAC BATTERY-POWERED SKATE-BOARDER. C. 1987.

MCDONALD'S PLAYGROUND ORNAMENTS FROM THE EIGHTIES.

HAMBURGER AIR-GLIDER. C. 1990.

BUILD A BETTER BURGER GAME. C. 1986.

A RARE BURGERTIME VIDEO ARCADE GAME. MANUFACTURED IN 1982 BY THE BALLY MIDWAY COMPANY.

HAMBURGER ORGAN. C. 1985.

PLEASE DON'T EAT THE BURGERS, CHILDREN. THE PLAY-DOH BURGER AND MALT SHOP MAKES "PRETEND BURGERS." C. 1981.

FAST FOOD YO-YO. C. 1989.

FUTUREBURGER

BIGGER, FASTER, BETTER?

The modern burger has become a bizarre beast of infinite shapes, sizes, and configurations. From Tri-burgers—triangular shaped burger patties served on crescent rolls—to Burger Booms—both the burger and the bun are shaped like boomerangs (the menu claimed "it gets you coming and going")—to Rocket-burgers and Raisin-burgers, these otherworldly creations are often frightfully inappropriate.

In the Eighties, giant overdressed burgers were in vogue as a spate of pricey gourmet burger chains including Red Robin, Flakey Jakes, Bonkers, and Fud-druckers sizzled across America serving burgers gar-

THE HIGH-TECH INSTANT BURGER COOKER WITH "DIRECT ENERGY TRANSFER" COOKS THE BURGERS FROM THE INSIDE OUT. PERFECT FOR TODAY'S SMOKE-FREE ENVIRONMENTS.

BOGUS BEEFLESS BURGERS WILL KEEP TRYING.

FULLY COOKED FROZEN MICROWAVE BURGERS. NOW WITH GOOD HOUSEKEEPING'S SEAL OF APPROVAL. TO REVIVE A FREEZE-DRIED HAMBURGER, JUST ADD WATER!

THE UNIVERSITY OF WISCONSIN'S THOMAS P. PHILIPS DEMONSTRATES THE AMAZING HAMBURGER ROBOT HE HELPED DEVELOP TO REDUCE THE COST OF BURGER-MAKING IN THE NINETIES.

nished with exotic accouterments including mango-chutney, guacamole, and goat cheese. This was not exactly a new approach, The Hamburger Hamlet had been specializing in gourmet burgers since they first opened in 1950 in Beverly Hills.

Although restaurant trade journals hailed the gourmet hamburger as the changemaker of 1984, these hefty, high-falutin' hamburgers did not transform the industry, and within two years many of its proponents scaled back operations drastically.

Today basic high-speed hamburgers continue to be a national priority. New burger chains such as Checkers and Rally's feature two drive-up windows and no indoor seating. They are essentially hamburger pit stops, ca-

IN THE FUTURISTIC FIFTIES, BURGER ESTABLISHMENTS SERVING BURGERS ON REMOTE-CONTROLLED MINIATURE TRAINS WERE POPULAR IN A NUMBER OF CITIES. AT THE HAMBURGER EXPRESS, HAMBURGER CHOO-CHOO, HAMBURGER JUNCTION, AND WHISTLE STOP RESTAURANTS, THE TRAINS TRAVELED WITH THEIR PRECIOUS CARGO FROM THE GRILL AREA TO A COUNTER IN FRONT. IN THIS 1952 PHOTO, ENGINEER-CHEF LESTER GOODMAN SETS THE WHEELS IN MOTION AT THE WHISTLE STOP IN CHICAGO.

THE HOT 'N NOW DOUBLE DRIVE-THRU IS NINETIES STATE-OF-THE-ART. THE EMPHASIS IS ON SPEED.

tering to the increasing number of burger consumers with just enough time to grab and go.

Meanwhile, burger-making robots have been hailed as "the first step toward a totally automated burger," and high-tech pushbutton hamburgers are as close as your grocer's freezer. These precooked, preconstructed microwavable marvels go from the deep freeze to the dinner plate in a matter of seconds giving new meaning to the term "fast food." For backpackers and astronauts freeze-dried hamburgers are now available.

Hamburger researchers have been working overtime perfecting a leaner breed of burger. In 1991 McDonald's replaced the McD.L.T. with the McLean Deluxe—a concoction with reduced fat and added seaweed, but light-burger technology has yet to spark a revolution in American hamburger habits.

Unfortunately there are also numerous mock-burger formulations available. The unremarkable turkey-burger is widespread, and natural food purveyors have promoted leaden veggie-burger cuisine for years. With names like Tofu Bliss-Burgers, and East of Eden Burgers these perverted patties contain no meat, just nutty things like walnuts, buckwheat groats,

THE BIGGEST BURGER THE WORLD HAS EVER SEEN REQUIRED A GRILL THE SIZE OF A 2-CAR GARAGE. IT WEIGHED IN AT 5,005 POUNDS AND FED 2,000 IN SEYMOUR, WISCONSIN, IN 1989.

ONLY THE BEST FOR MAN'S BEST FRIEND.

MODERN SPACE-AGE POLYMERS EXTEND CHEWING PLEASURE FOR POOCHES.

IN LOS ANGELES AND ACROSS AMERICA JOHNNY ROCKETS BRINGS
BURGERS BACK TO THE BASICS.

oat bran, bean curd, and sprouted barley. All are
very un-burgerlike, and are to be avoided.

After decades of "progress" in which mass-pro-
duced high-polished hamburgers have become the
norm, a tidal wave of trendy retro-burger palaces
with Fifties menus, music and motifs are making
a big splash. Offering a nostalgic alternative, restaurants such as Ed Debevic's and Johnny Rockets, place considerable emphasis on recreating the
period environment, and in some cases do a decent
job of delivering the goods.

IN 1964, THIS SPACED-OUT ROCKETBURGER RECIPE
UNITED TWO OF THE ERA'S GREATEST OBSESSIONS.

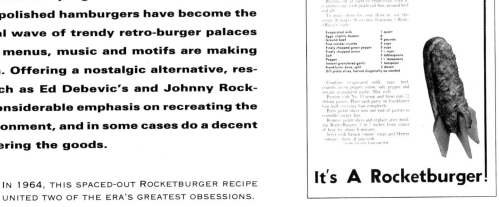

That unusual burger up there on the space
platform is a RocketBurger you can offer for
special appeal to your space-age kiddie customers.

Blasting off at right to rendezvous with it
is another one, with pickle tail fins, ground beef
and all.

To make them for your drive-in, use this
recipe. It makes 36 servings, featuring 2 RocketBurgers each.

Evaporated milk	1 quart
Eggs, slightly beaten	6
Ground beef	9 pounds
Fine cracker crumbs	3 cups
Finely chopped green pepper	2 cups
Finely chopped onion	1½ cups
Salt	3 tablespoons
Pepper	1½ teaspoons
Instant granulated garlic	1 teaspoon
Frankfurter buns, split	3 dozen
Dill pickle slices, halved diagonally as needed

Combine evaporated milk, eggs, beef,
crumbs, green pepper, onion, salt, pepper and
instant granulated garlic. Mix well.

Portion with No. 10 scoop and form into 72
oblong patties. Place each patty on frankfurter
bun half, covering bun completely.

Press pickle slices into one end of patties to
resemble rocket fins.

Remove pickle slices and replace after broiling RocketBurgers 3 in 5 inches from source
of heat for about 6 minutes.

Serve with Saturn (onion) rings and Meteor
(tomato) slices, if you wish.

Courtesy Carnation Evaporated Milk

It's A Rocketburger!

PERFECT BURGERS

AT HOME AND ON THE ROAD

AAAAAHHHH . . . PERFECT!!

The perfect burger is a vision to behold. The best hamburgers offer a cosmic experience on many levels; they are a pleasure to have and to hold. Getting your hands on one is another matter. Sad to say, there is no shortage of unremarkable burgers in today's world. The poor patties have suffered of late, as sacrifices made in the name of progress and profit repeatedly jeopardize their good standing, and impeccable reputations.

In the interest of good taste and the American Way, we present, herewith, a selection of America's finest burger emporiums. Establishments who have built a reputation on the power and the glory of their burgers. And for those with a penchant for the home-grown variety, a recipe for the perfect hamburger. It's as close as your own backyard.

FOR OVER TWENTY YEARS MANY CONSIDERED THE BURGERS PHYLIS MOFFET SERVED AT HAMBURG HEAVEN TO BE NEW YORK CITY'S FINEST. ESTABLISHED IN 1939, THERE WERE SIX LOCATIONS INCLUDING A TWENTY-FOUR-HOUR RESTAURANT IN THE EAST SIDE AIRLINES TERMINAL, WHERE THE MENU PROUDLY STATED THAT "THE GATES OF HEAVEN NEVER CLOSE."

ON THE ROAD

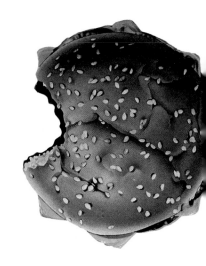

The eternal quest for the perfect burger ends here. From high-end to hole-in-the-wall, devout hamburger specialists provide a vital service to the community. Recommended by loyal customers and critics nationwide, these eateries deserve our whole-hearted support for their dedication to perfection.

ALABAMA:
IRONDALE—Hamburger Heaven, 1729 Crestwood Boulevard.
MONTGOMERY—Hamburger King, 132 S. Perry Street.

ALASKA:
ANCHORAGE—The Lucky Wishbone, 1033 E. Fifth Avenue.
ANCHORAGE—Arctic Roadrunner, 5300 Old Seward Highway.

ARIZONA:
SCOTTSDALE—Pischke's Paradise, 7217 E. First Street.

ARKANSAS:
PARAGOULD—Hamburger Station, 110 East Main Street.

CALIFORNIA:
EL CERRITO—Nib's Burgers, 1084 San Pablo Avenue.
LARKSPUR—Lark Creek Inn, 234 Magnolia Avenue.
LOS ANGELES—Tommy's, 2575 Beverly Boulevard.
LOS ANGELES—Gooey Louie's, 12630 Washington Place.
SAN FRANCISCO—Balboa Cafe, 3199 Fillmore Street.
SAN DIEGO—Doodle Burger, 3737 India Street.
Any In-N-Out Burger.

COLORADO:
ASPEN—Little Annie's, 517 East Hyman Avenue.
BOULDER—Tom's Tavern, 1047 Pearl Street.
DENVER—Ship Tavern, The Brown Palace Hotel, 321 17th Street.

CONNECTICUT:
BETHEL—The Sycamore, 282 Greenwood Avenue.
DANBURY—Chuck's Steak House, 20 Segar Street.
NEW HAVEN—Louis' Lunch, 261263 Crown Street.

DELAWARE:
NEWARK—Deer Park, 108 W. Main Street.
WILMINGTON—Charcoal Pit, Concord Pike.

DISTRICT OF COLUMBIA:
GEORGETOWN—Hamburger Hamlet, 3125 North Street, N.W.

FLORIDA:
HOLMES BEACH—Duffy's Tavern, 3901 Gulf Drive North.
ST. PETERSBURG—The Chattaway, 358 22nd Avenue South.
SOUTH PASADENA—Ted Peters, 1350 Pasadena Avenue.

GEORGIA:
ATLANTA—Manuel's Tavern, 602 North Highland.
LA GRANGE—Charlie Joseph's, 128 Bull Street.

HAWAII:
ANAHOLA—Ono-Char Burger, Kuhio Highway, Kaua'i.
HONOLULU—Hamburger Mary's, 2109 Kuhio Avenue, Oahu.

IDAHO:
COEUR D'ALENE—Hudson's, 207 Sherman Avenue.

ILLINOIS:
CHICAGO—Johnny Rockets, 801 N. Rush Street.
CHICAGO—International Club, Drake Hotel, 140 E. Walton Street.
GLENVIEW—Hackney's on Harms, 1241 Harms Road.
PEORIA—Maid-Rite Hamburgers, 1200 W. Main Street.

INDIANA:
INDIANAPOLIS—Dodd's, 110 W. Washington Street.
MISHAWAKA—Bonnie Doon's, 109 East Fourth Street.

IOWA:
DES MOINES—Drake Diner, 1111 25th Street.
OTTUMWA—The Canteen, 112 E. Second Street.
WEST DES MOINES—Maxie's, 1311 Grand Avenue.

KANSAS:
SALINA—Cozy Inn, 108 North Seventh Street.
TOPEKA—Seabrook Tavern and Grill, 2105 Mission Street.

KENTUCKY:
LOUISVILLE—Kaelin's, 1801 Newburg Road.
LOUISVILLE—Ollie's Trolley, 978 S. Third Street.

TOMMY'S CHILI BURGER IS LEGENDARY IN LOS ANGELES. FOUNDER TOM KOULAX OUTSIDE HIS FIRST STAND ON BEVERLY BOULEVARD ABOUT 1946.

LOUISIANA:
HARVEY—Ruby Red's, 1525 Lapaco.
NEW ORLEANS—Port O'Call, 838 Esplanade Avenue.
MAINE:
PORTLAND—Ruby's Choice, 116 Free Street.
MARYLAND:
TOWSON—Little Tavern, 1513 E. Joppa Road.
MASSACHUSETTS:
BOSTON—Tim's Tavern, 329 Columbus Avenue.
CAMBRIDGE—Harvest Restaurant, 44 Brattle Street.
STOCKBRIDGE—Red Lion Inn, Main Street.
MICHIGAN:
READING—Ray's Tavern, 114 North Main Street.
ROYAL OAK—Little Hut, 1128 South Main Street.
MINNESOTA:
INVER GROVE—White Castle, 4515 S. Robert Street.
MANKATO—Hamburger Heaven, 1021 Madison Street.
MISSISSIPPI:
HOLLY SPRINGS—Phillip's Grocery, 541 E. Van Dorn Avenue.
MISSOURI:
COLUMBIA—Booche's Billiard Hall, 110 S. Ninth Street.
KANSAS CITY—Jimmy's Jigger, 1823 W. 39th Street.
SEDALIA—The Wheel Inn, 1800 W. Broadway.
MONTANA:
BILLINGS—Tiny's Tavern, 323 N. 24th Street.
NEBRASKA:
HARRISON—Sioux Sundries, Second and Main Street.
NEVADA:
CARSON CITY—Clancy's Cork & Cue, 316 East Winnie Lane.
NEW HAMPSHIRE:
HANOVER—Molly's Balloon, 43 S. Main Street.

IN KANSAS, THE COZY INN HAS GRILLED THEIR LITTLE "COZIES" WITH ONIONS SINCE 1922.

NEW JERSEY:
HACKENSACK—White Manna Diner, 358 River Street.
NEW MEXICO:
SAN ANTONIO—The Owl Bar and Cafe, Main Street.
NEW YORK:
BREWSTER—The Red Rooster, Route 22.
EASTCHESTER—The Piper's Kilt, 433 White Plains Road.
NEW YORK CITY—All State Cafe, 250 W. 72nd Street.
NEW YORK CITY—Taste of the Apple, 1000 Second Avenue.
NEW YORK CITY—The 21 Club, 21 W. 52nd Street.
SHELTER ISLAND—Chequit Inn, 23 Grand Avenue.
NORTH CAROLINA:
ELIZABETHTOWN—Melvin's Restaurant, Broad Street.
WRIGHTSVILLE BEACH—The Dockside, 1308 Airlie Road.
NORTH DAKOTA:
BISMARCK—Cock and Bull Dakota Burgers, 900 Expressway.
OHIO:
LIMA—Kewpee's Hamburgers, 111 North Elizabeth Street.
OKLAHOMA:
OKLAHOMA CITY—Johnnie's, 2652 W. Britton Street.
OKLAHOMA CITY—The Split T Bar, 5701 N. Western.

OREGON:
O'BRIEN—Cave's Country Kitchen, 33095 Redwood Hwy.
PORTLAND—Perry's, 2401 N.E. Fremont Street.
PENNSYLVANIA:
BLOOMFIELD—Tessaro's, 4601 Liberty Ave.
POTTSVILLE—The Coney Island, 23rd and W. Market Street.
RHODE ISLAND:
PROVIDENCE—Leon's On Broadway, 500 Broadway.
PROVIDENCE—The Rhumb Line, 62 Bridge Street.
SOUTH CAROLINA:
SPARTANBURG—The Beacon Drive-in, 255 Reidville Road.
SOUTH DAKOTA:
SIOUX FALLS—Fuddrucker's, 3101 W. 41st Street.
TENNESSEE:
NASHVILLE—Brown's Diner, 2102 Blair Boulevard.
NASHVILLE—Eddie's Eat Shop, 3309 Nolensville Pike.

SOME OF THE BEST BURGERS IN NEW YORK STATE ARE SOLD AT THE RED ROOSTER ON ROUTE 22 IN BREWSTER. AN AUTHENTIC FIFTIES WALK-UP WITH VERY HIGH STANDARDS.

TEXAS:
AUSTIN—Mad Dog and Beans, 512 W. 24th Street.
DALLAS—Keller's Drive-in, 3766 Samuell's Blvd.
DALLAS—Theo's Diner, 111 S. Hall Street.
HOUSTON—The Snack Bar at Kroger's, 3300 Montrose Street.
HOUSTON—Avalon Drug and Diner, 2518 Kirby Street.
UTAH:
DRAPER—Iceberg Drive-In, 673 E. 12300 South.
SALT LAKE CITY—Cotton Bottoms Inn, 2820 E. 6200 South.
VERMONT:
ST. JOHNSBURY—Anthony's, 50 Railroad Street.
VIRGINIA:
NEWPORT NEWS—What-A-Burger, 6117 Jefferson Avenue.
NORFOLK—Kelly's Tavern, 1408 Colley Avenue.
WASHINGTON:
SEATTLE—Two Bell's Tavern, 2313 Fourth Avenue.
WALLA WALLA—The Iceberg, 616 W. Birch Street.
WEST VIRGINIA:
CHARLESTON—Quarrier Diner, 1022 Quarrier Street.
WISCONSIN:
MADISON—Dotty Dumpling's, 116 N. Fairchild Street.
LUCK—Luck-E Tavern, 211 S. Main Street.
WYOMING:
LANDER—Judd's Grub Drive-In, 634 Main Street.

HOMESTYLE

VERY IMPORTANT! FIND YOURSELF A REPUTABLE BUTCHER WITH A FACE YOU CAN TRUST.

The secret of a Heavenly Hamburger is fresh meat ground the same day and cooked to order the old-fashioned way. Pure and simple.

The meat should be lean but not too lean. For the tastiest burgers, a fat content between 20 and 25 percent is ideal because the best burgers are sloppy four-napkin affairs. Ask your butcher for choice chuck steak and have him grind it twice, first through a coarse plate and then through a fine one. Some aficionados like to grind the meat themselves—a "hands-on" approach that enriches the experience but is not crucial. If you grind the meat yourself, trim away the excess fat and cut the meat into medium size chunks. Chill the meat in the freezer for fifteen minutes to prevent stringiness during grinding.

When forming the patties, it is very important not to overhandle the meat. The less molding and shaping, the more flavorful and juicy the burger. Press the meat just enough to hold the patties together. Don't mix the seasoning into the meat, add it while cooking or after you have removed it from the grill. And never use your spatula to flatten the patties during cooking. Let them sizzle in peace, and be sure to flip them only once.

When preparing a hamburger at home, absolute perfection is within everyone's reach, as this recipe makes deliciously clear.

WORLD'S BEST BURGERS

1½ lbs freshly ground choice chuck steak
Hamburger buns from the bakery (if available)
Salt and freshly ground pepper
Olive oil (or vegetable oil)
American cheese slices (optional)

Exercising a light touch, form the meat into six round patties 4 inches in diameter and about 1 inch thick. Light the coals and allow the flames to subside. Before placing the grill over the coals, soak a paper napkin with olive oil and rub the cold grill with it. When the charcoal is covered with gray ash, place the meat on the grill 4 inches from the fire. Cook for about 4 minutes until well seared on one side. Lightly brush the tops with olive oil and sprinkle each patty with salt and fresh pepper. Carefully flip the patty, add cheese, and grill about 4 minutes longer, or to the desired degree of doneness. During the last 2 minutes of cooking, place the buns on the grill and allow them to brown. Remove toasted buns and burgers. Apply toppings to suit individual taste. YIELD: Six hamburgers

AND IF IT RAINS: Perfect burgers should be cooked on the grill, but you can pan-broil them. Heat a heavy skillet till very hot. Brush patties lightly with oil, add to pan, and cook over medium-high heat for 3 minutes. Salt and pepper the tops, turn, and add cheese. Cook an additional 4 minutes or longer for well done.

SIDEKICKS

French fries are the burger's most famous companion and side dish. Thomas Jefferson first discovered them in France and brought them home to Monticello. Today, when eating out, burgers and fries are practically inseparable, but not so in the home. At the burger cookout, potato chips and potato salad are standard fare. Grandma might bring jello, and that's okay, too.

GARNISH GUIDE

The beauty of the perfect burger is that it allows for creative self-expression. Some prefer theirs chili-soaked, others wouldn't lay their hands on a baconless burger. To each their own. Condiments should complement without overwhelming the meat. Here are the building blocks of a really boss burger.

ICEBERG LETTUCE LEAVES (not shredded): They just look and crunch right. No other green thing will do.

SLICED TOMATOES: Vine-ripened, red ones. If there is still such a thing available.

ONIONS: Chopped, sliced, raw, or grilled. The Tartars tried them. The rest is history.

PICKLES: "Hamburger dill chips" were bred for this specific purpose. They bring a crisp touch of tang.

KETCHUP: In moderation, adds color and balance. Heinz slow-pouring bottled brand is the accepted standard.

MUSTARD: A tiny bit for tartness. Bright yellow and made in America only. None of this "gray" stuff.

MAYONNAISE: To fuse the "salad elements." The deluxe mayonnaise, lettuce, and tomato burger caught on in California in the fifties, and is considered by many to be the hamburger in its most highly evolved state.

CHEESE: Smooth, modern, and perfectly orange, American cheese was born to adorn the burger. In 1924 California grill chef Lionel Sternberger concocted the first "cheese hamburger" in Pasadena's The Rite Spot restaurant.

BUNS: The supermarket variety is fine as long as they're not too spongy. Many bakeries offer a sturdier version.

T H A N K Y O U !

BOB AND SUE QUIMBY, PROPRIETORS, FOSTER'S FRIENDLY HAMBURGERS.
MISHAWAKA, INDIANA, 1982.

I would like to thank John Baeder whose boundless enthusiasm and generous contributions greatly enrich this project. Philip Langdon offered vital guidance, in addition to the wealth of information contained in his authoritative volume *Orange Roofs Golden Arches*. Michael Groen lent his photographic expertise and a great deal of his time. Fran Strauss and Carol Thompson provided insight and assistance throughout the long process. Victor Weaver helped to hone the vision. Steven Izenhour shared his White Tower wisdom. Thanks to Debby Kline, Jane Leahy, and White Castle Systems for taking the time to unearth their glorious treasures for me. I am especially grateful for the assistance and encouragement of Thomas Steele, Richard Gutman, Alan Hess, Jim Heimann, and Eldon Davis, whose work has been a considerable source of inspiration for me over the years. David Slovic, Ken Brown, Pam Colglazier, Tod Swarmstedt, Pierce Reibsamen, and Robert E. Wildman enhanced these pages immeasurably with their photographic contributions. My sincere appreciation and admiration for lifetime Hamburger Men: Richard McDonald and Bob Wian (the legends), David Edgerton, Frank P. Thomas, Martin Cable, Everett Williams, Thomas Dolly, and Boe Messet, who all lived this incredible story and took time out to tell me the tale. Thanks to Eleanor Cohan, Ellen Gartrell, Jane Karr, and Philip Horowitz for their superb research. Brenda McCallum and Jean Geist facilitated my work at Bowling Green State University's Popular Culture Library. Jeff Weinstein offered direction. Lyle Sumerix, Terry DeShone, Bob Greene, and Lewie Chambers helped get the ball rolling. Martha Kaplan, my marvelous editor and guiding light, made it all happen. I am forever grateful to the following hamburger helpers who gave freely of their time and burgers: Becky Luedeke, Lorin Katz, Patrick Pacheco, André De Shields, Chico Kasinoir, Terry Seese, Rich Seidelman, Lester and Teresa Silva, Gerry Geddes, Dan Kimpel, Yuji Nishimoto, Kim Kachner, Rick Fiala, Brad Ensminger, Dana White, Michael Hinders, Liz Baron, Mazin and Heather Sami, Harry Sperl, Lance Golba, Raymond Patterson, Paul Schnee, Karen Maier, Dottie Eden, Chris Nichols, and The Tennysons. Rodney Lipp and Brant Mewborne guided this work in spirit. And Jay Brown introduced me to The Red Rooster. His contribution cannot be measured.

ILLUSTRATIONS

J.J.C. Andrews: 93 (top).
Armet Davis Newlove: 38 (top right), 51 (bottom), 54–56.
Art Gallery of Ontario, Toronto: 108 (top).
The Athens Review: 19 (bottom).
John Baeder: 4, 14 (bottom), 18, 19 (top), 23, 33 (top), 69 (bottom).
British Museum of Natural History: 8, 10.
Lou Brooks: 127 (bottom right).
Ken Brown: 48 (bottom), 91 (bottom left).
Burger King Corporation: 77.
Martin Cable: 37 (top).
Cambridge Historical Commission: 39 (top).
Caufield and Shook Collection, University of Louisville Photographic Archives: 23 (top).
Pam Colglazier: 38 (center), 41 (top), 45, 90 (top right).
Cossette Communication-Marketing: 102 (top).
Steve Fitch: 91 (bottom right).
Foodmaker, Inc.: 64 (bottom right), 78 (top), 90 (top).
Michael Groen: 3, 87 (center), 110–117, 119 (bottom).
Richard Gutman: 14 (top), 73 (top), 90 (left center and bottom right), 93 (top right).
Richard Hailey, Texas Pig Stands: 36, 44 (bottom).
Hardee's Food Systems, Inc.: 65 (top), 71 (top).
The Huntington Library: 37 (center).
J. Walter Thompson Company Archives, Duke University/Burger King Corporation: 52 (bottom), 84 (top left).
Kansas State Historical Society: 13.
Collection of Judy Kismits: 17.
Karen Koshgarian: 64 (top and bottom).
Sara Krulwich/NYT Pictures: 119 (top).
Lake County Museum, Curt Teich Collection: 50 (top), 65 (bottom), 76 (top left).
Collection of Philip Langdon: 30 (center).
Los Angeles Public Library, Security Pacific National Bank Collection: 37 (bottom).
Dick Luria: 126.
John Margolies/Esto: 92 (top).
Richard McDonald: 61.
Larry McEntire: 42.
Collection of Richard McLay: 43 (top).
Gary McQuire, courtesy Keiler and Company: 88 (center).
O.K. Harris Works of Art, NYC: 108 (bottom right).
National Car Rental: 121 (top).
Northern Indiana Historical Society: 90 (top left).
Outdoor Advertising Association of America, Fairleigh Dickinson University: 93 (bottom left), 100 (top and right), 101 (right).
Patrick Media, courtesy Joel Byron: 76 (center).
Raymond Patterson: 92 (right).
Peter Palombi: 124 (top right).
Petrified Photos: 122 (top).
QRS Sign Corporation: 36 (top).
Raymond Quiel: 58.
Reibsamen Nickels and Rex, George Szanik Photography: 40, 53 (bottom).
Robert Risko: 105, 127 (bottom left).
Collection of Richard Seidelman: 59, 86 (bottom left).
Sign of the Times magazine: 72, 73 (center and right).
Collection of Lester Silva: 29 (bottom), 30 (top right and bottom), 36 (bottom), 57, 88 (bottom).
David Slovic: 38 (top), 90 (top, inset).
Steve Soelberg Collection: 43 (bottom).
Randy South: 1.
Ken Spencer/Newsday: 63.
Steak n' Shake: 41 (bottom).
George Tames/NYT Pictures: 86 (bottom center).
Collection of Lisa Tennyson: 78 (bottom).
Jeffrey Tennyson: 5, 6, 10 (bottom), 15 (left), 32, 33 (bottom), 38 (bottom), 49 (bottom), 52, 64 (bottom), 76 (top), 84 (top right), 89, (left center, bottom left, right center), 85 (top), 93 (bottom right), 94, 98, 99, 100 (bottom left), 101 (top, bottom left), 103, 123, 128.
Heinz Tiede: 125 (right).
Tombrock Corporation: 28, 31, 35, 43, 80 (top).
Wendy's International: 80, 81, 85 (top).
White Castle System, Inc.: 20–22, 23 (bottom), 25.
Wide World: 119 (bottom).
Robert E. Wildman: 69 (top).

All efforts have been made to identify and contact sources represented in this book. Any illustration unknowingly uncredited will be acknowledged in later editions.